Sciences
Enginee
Medicii

MW00781159

A Plan to Promote Defense Research at Minority-Serving Institutions

Andrea Christelle, Erin Lynch, and
André N. Porter, *Editors*

Committee on the Development of
a Plan to Promote Defense Research
at Historically Black Colleges and
Universities, Tribal Colleges and
Universities, Hispanic-Serving
Institutions, and Other
Minority-Serving Institutions

Board on Higher Education
and Workforce

Policy and Global Affairs

Consensus Study Report

NATIONAL ACADEMIES PRESS 500 Fifth Street, NW Washington, DC 20001

This activity was supported by a contract between the National Academy of Sciences and the U.S. Department of Defense. Any opinions, findings, conclusions, or recommendations expressed in this publication do not necessarily reflect the views of any organization or agency that provided support for the project.

International Standard Book Number-13: 978-0-309-72206-3
International Standard Book Number-10: 0-309-72206-3
Digital Object Identifier: https://doi.org/10.17226/27838
Library of Congress Control Number: 2024946770

This publication is available from the National Academies Press, 500 Fifth Street, NW, Keck 360, Washington, DC 20001; (800) 624-6242; http://www.nap.edu.

Copyright 2024 by the National Academy of Sciences. National Academies of Sciences, Engineering, and Medicine and National Academies Press and the graphical logos for each are all trademarks of the National Academy of Sciences. All rights reserved.

Printed in the United States of America.

Suggested citation: National Academies of Sciences, Engineering, and Medicine. 2024. *A Plan to Promote Defense Research at Minority-Serving Institutions.* Washington, DC: National Academies Press. https://doi.org/10.17226/27838.[1]

---

[1] This title was modified after release of the report to the study sponsor to more accurately represent the original congressional intent.

The **National Academy of Sciences** was established in 1863 by an Act of Congress, signed by President Lincoln, as a private, nongovernmental institution to advise the nation on issues related to science and technology. Members are elected by their peers for outstanding contributions to research. Dr. Marcia McNutt is president.

The **National Academy of Engineering** was established in 1964 under the charter of the National Academy of Sciences to bring the practices of engineering to advising the nation. Members are elected by their peers for extraordinary contributions to engineering. Dr. John L. Anderson is president.

The **National Academy of Medicine** (formerly the Institute of Medicine) was established in 1970 under the charter of the National Academy of Sciences to advise the nation on medical and health issues. Members are elected by their peers for distinguished contributions to medicine and health. Dr. Victor J. Dzau is president.

The three Academies work together as the **National Academies of Sciences, Engineering, and Medicine** to provide independent, objective analysis and advice to the nation and conduct other activities to solve complex problems and inform public policy decisions. The National Academies also encourage education and research, recognize outstanding contributions to knowledge, and increase public understanding in matters of science, engineering, and medicine.

Learn more about the National Academies of Sciences, Engineering, and Medicine at **www.nationalacademies.org**.

Consensus Study Reports published by the National Academies of Sciences, Engineering, and Medicine document the evidence-based consensus on the study's statement of task by an authoring committee of experts. Reports typically include findings, conclusions, and recommendations based on information gathered by the committee and the committee's deliberations. Each report has been subjected to a rigorous and independent peer-review process and it represents the position of the National Academies on the statement of task.

Proceedings published by the National Academies of Sciences, Engineering, and Medicine chronicle the presentations and discussions at a workshop, symposium, or other event convened by the National Academies. The statements and opinions contained in proceedings are those of the participants and are not endorsed by other participants, the planning committee, or the National Academies.

Rapid Expert Consultations published by the National Academies of Sciences, Engineering, and Medicine are authored by subject-matter experts on narrowly focused topics that can be supported by a body of evidence. The discussions contained in rapid expert consultations are considered those of the authors and do not contain policy recommendations. Rapid expert consultations are reviewed by the institution before release.

For information about other products and activities of the National Academies, please visit www.nationalacademies.org/about/whatwedo.

COMMITTEE ON THE DEVELOPMENT OF A PLAN TO PROMOTE DEFENSE RESEARCH AT HISTORICALLY BLACK COLLEGES AND UNIVERSITIES, TRIBAL COLLEGES AND UNIVERSITIES, HISPANIC-SERVING INSTITUTIONS, AND OTHER MINORITY-SERVING INSTITUTIONS

ANDREA CHRISTELLE (*Co-Chair*), Vice Provost of Research, Diné College
ERIN LYNCH (*Co-Chair*), President, The Quality Education for Minorities Network
NADYA T. BLISS, Executive Director and Professor of Practice, Global Security Initiative, Arizona State University
ROBERT D. BRAUN (NAE), Head, Space Exploration, Johns Hopkins Applied Physics Laboratory
BRIAN K. CHAPPELL, Research Staff Member, Nuclear Weapons Strategy and Policy, Institute for Defense Analyses
PAUL T. DEADERICK, Senior Project Leader, The Aerospace Corporation
BRUCE H. DUNSON, President, Metrica, Inc.
ERICK C. JONES, Former Dean, College of Engineering and Professor of Mechanical Engineering, University of Nevada, Reno
KEITH A. McGEE, Associate Professor, Biology, Alcorn State University
ERIC R. MUTH, Vice Chancellor, Division of Research and Economic Development, North Carolina Agricultural and Technical State University
ANNA M. QUIDER, Founder and Principal, The Quider Group
AARON M. SCHUTT, President/CEO, Doyon, Limited
SHARON TETTEGAH, Professor and Director, Center for Black Studies Research, University of California, Santa Barbara (*until March 27, 2024*)
C. REYNOLD VERRET, President, Xavier University of Louisiana

Study Staff

ANDRÉ N. PORTER, Study Director and Senior Program Officer, Board on Higher Education and Workforce
MARIA LUND DAHLBERG, Board Director, Board on Higher Education and Workforce

JOHN VERAS, Associate Program Officer, Board on Higher Education and Workforce

ANDREA DALAGAN, Senior Program Assistant, Board on Higher Education and Workforce

JUSTIN WANG, Christine Mirzayan Science & Technology Policy Graduate Fellow, Board on Higher Education and Workforce

CLARA HARVEY-SAVAGE, Senior Finance Business Partner, Policy and Global Affairs

CYRIL LEE, Finance Business Partner, Policy and Global Affairs

Consultants

PAULA T. WHITACRE, Writer

RUBY (RUISHAN) ZHANG, Research Assistant and Ph.D. Candidate, Harvard University

BOARD ON HIGHER EDUCATION AND WORKFORCE

MARIELENA DeSANCTIS (*Co-Chair*), President, Community College of Denver

LAMONT R. TERRELL (*Co-Chair*), Diversity, Equity, and Inclusion Lead, GSK

RAJEEV DAROLIA, Wendell H. Ford Professorship in Public Policy and Professor of Public Policy and Economics, University of Kentucky

JOAN FERRINI-MUNDY, President, University of Maine and University of Maine at Machias; Vice Chancellor for Research and Innovation, University of Maine System

MATTHEW HORA, Associate Professor of Adult and Higher Education and Founding Director, Center for Research on College-Workforce Transitions, University of Wisconsin–Madison

BRANDY HUDERSON, Assistant Professor of Biology, University of the District of Columbia; Diversity, Equity, and Inclusion Consultant and Data Analyst, Avent Diversity Consulting

TASHA R. INNISS, Associate Provost for Research, Office of Research, Innovation, and Collaboration, Spelman College

TRACIE LATTIMORE, Executive Director, Health Readiness Policy & Oversight, Office of the U.S. Secretary of Defense

HIRONAO OKAHANA, Assistant Vice President and Executive Director, Education Futures Lab, American Council on Education

JOERG C. SCHLATTERER, Director, Scientific Advancement, Office of Research Grants, American Chemical Society

KATE E. STOLL, Project Director, Center for Scientific Evidence in Public Issues, American Association for the Advancement of Science

MEGHNA TARE, Chief Sustainability Officer, University of Texas at Arlington

ZAKIYA WILSON-KENNEDY, Ron and Dr. Mary Neal Distinguished Associate Professor of Chemistry Education and Associate Dean for Academic Innovation and Engagement, College of Science, Louisiana State University

JOSH WYNER, Executive Director, Aspen Institute College Excellence Program; Vice President, Aspen Institute

Staff

MARIA LUND DAHLBERG, Director
ANDREA DALAGAN, Senior Program Assistant
ANDRÉ N. PORTER, Senior Program Officer
KARLA RILEY, Senior Program Assistant
JOHN VERAS, Associate Program Officer
MELISSA E. WYNN, Program Officer

Reviewers

This Consensus Study Report was reviewed in draft form by individuals chosen for their diverse perspectives and technical expertise. The purpose of this independent review is to provide candid and critical comments that will assist the National Academies of Sciences, Engineering, and Medicine in making each published report as sound as possible and to ensure that it meets the institutional standards for quality, objectivity, evidence, and responsiveness to the study charge. The review comments and draft manuscript remain confidential to protect the integrity of the deliberative process.

We thank the following individuals for their review of this report:

KIRAN BHAGANAGAR, The University of Texas at San Antonio
EMILY BIGGANE, United Tribes Technical College
CHARLES JOHNSON-BEY, Booz Allen Hamilton
MICHELLE PENN-MARSHALL, Texas Southern University
JARET RIDDICK, Georgetown University
JAGANNATHAN SANKAR, North Carolina Agricultural and
    Technical State University
HELEN TURNER, Chaminade University of Honolulu
STEPHANIE YOUNG, RAND Corporation

Although the reviewers listed above provided many constructive comments and suggestions, they were not asked to endorse the conclusions or recommendations of this report, nor did they see the final draft before its release. The review of this report was overseen by **EDWARD LAZOWSKA**, University of Washington, and **LESTER LYLES**, Independent Consultant. They were responsible for making certain that an independent examination of this report was carried out in accordance with the standards of the National Academies and that all review comments were carefully considered. Responsibility for the final content rests entirely with the authoring committee and the National Academies.

Contents

APPENDIXES

Boxes, Figures, and Tables

BOXES

FIGURES

TABLES

Preface

In recent years, the landscape of higher education has witnessed a growing recognition of the vital role played by minority-serving institutions (MSIs) in shaping the nation's academic, research, and innovation ecosystems. Institutions designated as Minority-Serving represent 25 percent of all colleges and universities in the United States[1] and 37 percent of all public colleges and universities in the country. Predicted shifts in the national demographics suggest the potential for more MSIs emerging, making their access to and engagement in the national research and development (R&D) ecosystem critically important to the national economy, innovation development, and national security. While our free society is threatened by increasingly capable global adversaries, to support the Department of Defense (DOD) mission, it becomes imperative to engage and explore a wider range of institutions and human capital to develop complex solutions to defeat the threat. This volume delves into four key aspects of government engagement with MSIs and their impact on research, development in context of the capabilities of these institutions, and decision-making processes that contribute to a path forward for these organizations.

Foundationally, this report presents an assessment for MSIs but acknowledges the historic differences in asset access for different types of MSIs. Historically Black Colleges and Universities (HBCUs), per Department of Education guidelines, are the only type of college and university

---

[1] This excludes Carnegie Classified Special Focus Two-Year Schools.

not expected to increase in numbers based on demographic shift.[2] Also, as defined by the Higher Education Act of 1965, the Tribal Colleges and Universities designation is predicated on enrollment numbers and tribal affiliation. Asian American and Native American Pacific Islander-Serving Institutions, Hispanic-Serving Institutions, and Predominately Black Institutions are the only MSI classifications without explicit definitions related to the year of establishment or cultural affiliation. As such this study recognizes the historic under-resourcing of MSIs (McCambly and Colyvas, 2022) in context of those institutions historically founded as institutions for the education of racial and ethnic minority groups and those that have evolved into institutions educating racial and ethnic minorities based on enrollment shifts. This study speaks to the contextual differences in relation to DOD's response to support the variety of MSIs through six sections.

MSIs, like all our nation's universities, contribute significantly to society in many ways, including advancing knowledge, educating our population, and serving the public good. The committee's statement of task focuses narrowly on assessing the way MSIs can and do contribute to DOD research. It is important to point out that there is not a one-size-fits-all answer to this question nor does the committee assume that all MSIs should contribute to DOD research. As such, the degree to which the committee's findings and recommendations apply to each MSI is a function of the strategic interest of that institution in DOD research.

Chapter 2, "Government Engagement with Minority-Serving Institutions: History and Common Themes from Previous Reports," serves as a foundational exploration of the historic interactions between government entities and MSIs. By examining past reports and initiatives, this chapter illuminates common themes, challenges, and successes in government-MSI relationships, providing essential context for understanding the current landscape. Recommendations for this study related to the findings of this chapter are grounded in the concept of relationship building on the part of DOD and MSIs interested in conducting research to support the DOD mission.

Chapter 3, "Outlining Opportunities at MSIs: An Assessment of the Capabilities of Minority-Serving Institutions," provides a comprehensive assessment of the capabilities and potential of MSIs. Through a systematic examination of MSI resources, expertise, and infrastructure, this chapter aims to highlight the unique strengths and opportunities that MSIs offer in

---

[2] HBCUs had to be established before 1964 according to the Higher Education Act of 1965.

advancing research, innovation, and workforce development across diverse DOD-related fields. Recommendations for this study related to Chapter 3 findings are grounded in the qualitative evidence that emerged through public meetings and literature.

Chapter 4, "Department of Defense and Other Federal Support for Research and Development," delves into the critical role played by federal agencies, particularly the DOD, in supporting R&D activities at MSIs. By analyzing existing programs, funding mechanisms, and collaborative initiatives, this chapter elucidates the ways in which federal support catalyzes innovation and knowledge creation within the MSI community. Recommendations specific to Chapter 4 are grounded in the committee's research and analysis of currently available data.

Finally, Chapter 5, "Setting a Path Forward for Assessment and Decision-Making," outlines strategies and frameworks for enhancing assessment practices and decision-making processes related to government engagement with MSIs. By synthesizing insights from previous chapters and drawing on best practices from diverse stakeholders, this chapter proposes actionable recommendations for policymakers, institutional leaders, and stakeholders to foster more effective partnerships and outcomes. Recommendations are drawn from the learnings across all chapters and are framed in a manner that could be actionable for DOD and MSIs.

As we navigate the complexities and opportunities inherent in government-MSI collaborations, this volume seeks to inform and inspire dialogue, action, and innovation. By harnessing the collective wisdom and expertise of scholars, policymakers, practitioners, and MSI stakeholders, we aim to advance a shared vision of inclusive excellence and transformative impact in higher education, national security, innovation, and the prosperity of the nation.

Andrea Christelle and Erin Lynch, *Co-Chairs*
Committee on the Development of a Plan to
Promote Defense Research at Historically Black
Colleges and Universities, Tribal Colleges and
Universities, Hispanic-Serving Institutions,
and Other Minority-Serving Institutions

REFERENCE

McCambly, H., and J.A. Colyvas. 2022. Institutionalizing inequity anew: Grantmaking and racialized postsecondary organizations. *The Review of Higher Education*, 46(1), 67-107.

Acronyms and Abbreviations

AANAPISI	Asian American and Native American Pacific Islander-Serving Institutions
API	Application programming interface
ARL	Army Research Laboratory
CIP	Classification of Instructional Programs
COGR	Council on Government Relations
CTA	Critical Technology Area
DARPA	Defense Advanced Research Projects Agency
DOD	Department of Defense
DOE	Department of Energy
DTRA	Defense Threat Reduction Agency
DURIP	Defense University Research Instrumentation Program
ETS	Educational Testing Service
F&A	Facilities and administration costs
FAIR	Funding for Accelerated, Inclusive Research (DOE program)
FFRDC	Federally Funded Research and Development Center
FOA	Funding Opportunity Announcement

GRANTED	Growing Research Access for Nationally Transformative Equity and Diversity (NSF program)
HAIANE	High American Indian and Alaska Native Enrolling
HBCU	Historically Black College and University
HERD	Higher Education Research and Development Survey
HHE	High Hispanic Enrollment (institution)
HSI	Hispanic-Serving Institution
IDC	Indirect cost
IHE	Institution of higher education
IPEDS	Integrated Postsecondary Education Data System
MI	Minority Institution
MIRA	Maximizing Investigators' Research Award (NIH program)
MOSAIC	Maximizing Opportunities for Scientific and Academic Independent Careers (NIH program)
MRI	Major Research Instrumentation (NSF dataset)
MSI	Minority-Serving Institution
MTDC	Modified Total Direct Costs
MURI	Multidisciplinary University Research Initiative
NASA	National Aeronautics and Space Administration
NCES	National Center for Education Statistics
NDAA	National Defense Authorization Act
NIGMS	National Institute of General Medical Sciences
NIH	National Institutes of Health
NSF	National Science Foundation
ONR	Office of Naval Research
PM	Program manager
PUI	Primarily undergraduate institution
R&D	Research and development
RDT&E	Research, development, test, and evaluation
RENEW	Reaching a New Energy Sciences Workforce (DOE program)
RFI	Request for Information

RFP   Request for Proposals

S&E   Science and engineering
S&T   Science and technology
SMART   Science, Mathematics, and Research for Transformation
               program
SMD   Science Mission Directorate (NASA)
STEM   Science, technology, engineering, and mathematics
SWOT   Strengths, Weaknesses, Opportunities, Threats

TCU   Tribal College and University

UARC   University Affiliated Research Center

Summary

Engaging the full breadth of talent in the United States is an important component of growing and sustaining dominance in research and development (R&D) and supporting national security into the future. By 2030, one-fifth of Americans will be above age 65 and at or nearing retirement from the workforce. Estimates of race and ethnic demographic changes between 2016 and 2030 show a decrease in the non-Hispanic white population and an increase in terms of both number and share of all other demographic groups (U.S. Census, 2018), and this trend will continue. These population shifts signal a citizenry and workforce that will be increasingly diverse. For the United States to maintain its global competitiveness and protect its security interests, targeted support is needed to cultivate talent from communities throughout the nation.

The federal government's investment in R&D supports strengthening the nation's competitiveness and security. The nation's more than 800 minority-serving institutions (MSIs) provide an impactful and cost-effective opportunity to focus on cultivating the current and future U.S. population for careers in science, technology, engineering, and mathematics (STEM), including in fields critical to the U.S. Department of Defense (DOD). Given the DOD's interest in biomedical research, this report incorporates medicine when referencing "STEM" disciplines as a component of scientific research.

STUDY CHARGE

In response to the National Defense Authorization Act (NDAA) for FY23 Sec. 233 and the NDAA for FY20 Sec. 220,[1] DOD approached the National Academies of Sciences, Engineering, and Medicine (the National Academies) to identify tangible frameworks for increasing the participation of MSIs in defense-related R&D and, where possible, identify the necessary mechanisms for elevating MSIs to R1 status (doctoral universities with very high research activity) on the Carnegie Classification of Institutions of Higher Education scale. To address this charge, the National Academies appointed a committee to do the following:

1. Summarize previous National Academies' reports on MSIs, including capacity development and engagement in U.S. R&D;
2. Assess the activities and investments necessary to, where possible, elevate additional MSIs to R1 status and increase their participation in defense-related R&D and industries; and
3. Identify goals, incentives, and metrics to measure MSI capacity to address DOD's needs in engineering, research, and development.

The committee held nine committee meetings and five open sessions in 2023. The open sessions were useful to investigate existing MSI engagement strategies across the DOD branches and R&D programs, as well as learn about opportunities for collaboration and support with University Affiliated Research Centers (UARCs) and Federally Funded Research and Development Centers (FFRDCs). The committee also invited speakers from other federal agency programs involved in data collection or addressing the various components of capacity development at emerging research institutions to understand their frameworks and funding structures and elucidate best practices to identify mechanisms that could be adapted for DOD. A representative from the American Council on Education briefed the committee on the forthcoming changes to the Carnegie Classifications to better understand the metrics that will inform the revision.

In addition, the committee conducted three site visits to receive candid feedback and develop an assessment of institutional capacity and

---

[1] Text - S.1605 - 117th Congress (2021-2022): National Defense Authorization Act for Fiscal Year 2022. (2021, December 27). https://www.congress.gov/bill/117th-congress/house-bill/7776/text for FY 2023 and https://www.congress.gov/116/plaws/publ92/PLAW-116publ92.pdf for FY 2020.

opportunities. The site visits represented three targeted institution types: a Historically Black College and University (HBCU), Tribal College and University (TCU), and Hispanic-Serving Institution (HSI), respectively Fayetteville State University, Diné College, and California State University at Bakersfield. Recognizing that each school is unique, and these schools do not capture all HBCUs, TCUs, or HSIs, the visits were invaluable to expose committee members to the on-the-ground experiences of leaders, administrators, faculty, and students, as well as to tour facilities and other infrastructure. All three are engaged in research but are below R2 (High Research Activity) on the Carnegie Classification, and one aim of the visits was to identify potential interventions for increasing capacity at diverse and often under-supported institutions. The committee also drew from previous National Academies' studies and from perspectives shared during the National Academies-led Town Hall series on building defense research capacity (NASEM, 2024).

The committee developed and distributed a Request for Information (RFI) publicly available through the National Academies' website and other channels. The goals of the RFI were to collect information on how MSIs broadly assess their current research, resources, and capabilities; determine their research aspirations in defense-related research and industries critical to U.S. national security; and learn how they currently engage with DOD.

MSI CONTEXT

The nation's first MSIs were the HBCUs that trace their origins prior to the Civil War. The decades following the Civil War saw a flourishing of newly established institutions, both public and private, dedicated to the education of the formerly enslaved and their descendants. There are now more than 100 HBCUs.

TCUs were established by individual Native American tribes "to strengthen reservations and tribal culture without assimilation," starting with Navajo Community College (now Diné College) in 1968. TCU-specific federal funding only began through the Tribally Controlled Community College Assistance Act of 1978. And although the original Morrill Act to create land-grant universities was funded through the granting of more than 10 million acres of land expropriated from Native American tribes, Congress did not grant TCUs status as land-grant institutions until 1994. There are now 35 TCUs that operate more than 90 campuses and other sites.

In addition to these two historically defined designations, legislation between 1992 and 2008 established criteria for five categories of enrollment-defined or enrollment-driven MSIs, beginning with HSIs in 1992. As the Latino population increases and more Latino students enroll in 2- and 4-year institutions, the number of HSIs has increased in the past few decades. As of this writing, there are about 600 HSIs, and many others are on the cusp of reaching the federally defined threshold.

There is substantial diversity among MSIs related to mission, size, resources, location, STEM programs, and other characteristics. TCUs, for example, generally are small institutions of several hundred students, and many are geographically remote. Some of the larger HSIs are in urban areas educating tens of thousands of students. Some MSIs are actively working to boost their research portfolio while others see their primary purpose in teaching and service to their communities. Across these differences, they share several characteristics. They provide a strong system of support to students, many of whom are the first in their families to go on to higher education. They educate talent in STEM, social sciences, and humanities in service to the domestic and international agenda of the United States. They represent an underutilized and underappreciated asset in particular in growing the STEM workforce (NASEM, 2019). Yet, they also have in common the reality that on both the federal and state levels, support to MSIs has lagged behind support to non-MSIs since the 19th century and through the present day.

Language in the study charge asked the committee to consider ways to increase the number of MSIs reaching R1 Carnegie status. The committee did so in the context of strengthening research at all institutions who have this aim, both those that may and may not become R1s. As a system for describing large, well-funded academic institutions, the Carnegie Classifications are well situated to provide a cursory assessment of the research capabilities of R1 and R2 institutions. However, the committee felt the Carnegie Classifications have fallen short in providing an assessment of the unique contributions that institutions that fall below the R1/R2 thresholds provide the U.S. R&D ecosystem. R1s account for approximately 4 percent of all U.S. institutions of higher education, which means that the vast majority of U.S. students pursuing undergraduate and postgraduate education do so at a non-R1 institution. Non-R1 institutions include a diversity of schools that serve rural communities, returning learners, Indigenous and African American communities, and other populations that have much to offer DOD. Robust R&D engagement occurs at non-R1s. Thus, while R1 and

R2 designation is important for many institutions, targeting resources to a broader array of MSIs will expand capacity and provide an opportunity to increase the diversity of perspectives engaging throughout the U.S. R&D landscape.

DOD AND OTHER FEDERAL SUPPORT FOR R&D

As noted, the federal government's investment in R&D strengthens the nation's competitiveness and security. The study focused on DOD but also looked at research supported by other agencies in service of the national security of the United States. It and other studies (e.g., NASEM, 2019, 2022) point to the competitive advantages of increasing the capacity of HBCUs, TCUs, HSIs, and other MSIs to conduct defense-related research and train the next generation of scientists. Among the advantages are to increase the talent pool of U.S citizens equipped to take on work that requires security clearances and to offer complementary areas of knowledge, innovation, and experience to the existing R&D ecosystem.

In FY 2023, Congress appropriated $144 billion to DOD for a pipeline of activity, known collectively as research, development, test, and evaluation (RDT&E). Within RDT&E, university science and technology (S&T) engagement typically occurs in three parts of the pipeline: Basic Research, Applied Research, and, to a lesser extent, Advanced Technology Development, which had a combined appropriation in FY 2023 of about $22.5 billion. Multiple entities manage these funds. They include the Departments of the Air Force, Army, and Navy; offices within the Office of the Secretary of Defense; and defense agencies such as the Defense Advanced Research Projects Agency (DARPA) and the Defense Threat Reduction Agency. In addition, through its present set of UARCs and FFRDCs, the DOD has a research network that spans most of the United States. Many UARCs and FFRDCs are located in regions of the country with relatively nearby TCUs, HBCUs, and/or other MSIs. Taking advantage of this relative proximity may be an opportunity for greater engagement by UARCs and FFRDCs with MSIs.

The committee noted that while most defense-related research has focused on STEM, the social sciences, humanities, and other disciplines have been shown to be important in addressing emerging mission needs that range from rapid adoption of autonomy to tackling the integrity of the information environment (NASEM, 2020). Moreover, some emerging challenges, such as those related to environmental and societal impacts of new technologies, fall into the specific and unique expertise of many MSIs that have not traditionally engaged with the DOD. This recognition offers another avenue for acceleration of MSI participation in defense-related research.

Universities that work successfully with the DOD have developed a unique set of administrative, infrastructure, and process capabilities, along with general awareness of mission needs. Even universities that have a record of funded research with other agencies such as the National Science Foundation often require a different set of resources to engage at scale with the DOD. Working on the DOD research requires relevant research infrastructure, different financial processes (e.g., related to contract rather than grant management), and, in some cases, specialized facilities. Many MSIs do not have the resources to meet these requirements in order to, for example, lessen faculty teaching loads or invest in sponsored program expertise. Overall, the variation across the DOD Request for Proposals/Funding Opportunity Announcement processes can likely contribute to lower submission rates by MSIs without the resources to navigate the system.

The military services and other entities do have programs that are either explicitly designed for MSIs or are particularly conducive to MSI participation. In addition, the locus for MSI engagement within the DOD is the Research and Education Program for Historically Black Colleges & Universities and Minority Institutions (MIs) within the Office of the Secretary of Defense. While the office has made strong contributions, its budget of about $100 million represents only 0.56 percent of the S&T budget.

Defense-related research is sponsored by other federal agencies, such as the National Institutes of Health (NIH), National Science Foundation, National Aeronautics and Space Administration, Environmental Protection Agency, and Department of Energy. They also sponsor research and scholarship at HBCUs, HSIs, and TCUs in domains useful to national security concerns. Examples include but are not limited to studies in materials science, microbiology, toxicology, and marine science and oceanography. Deficits in support and engagement of MSIs not only have been relevant to the DOD but also extend to other agencies. The study committee hosted representatives from several agencies and drew on discussions during the Town Hall series to better understand the breadth of interventions used across the federal government. While not exhaustive, agency representatives shared promising examples aimed at increasing the engagement of underinvested institutions, some of which can provide the DOD with potential frameworks to adopt through the development or reconfiguration of its programs.

SETTING A PATH FORWARD FOR ASSESSMENT AND DECISION-MAKING

Previous reports have spotlighted challenges with collecting and utilizing data and operationalizing frameworks that effectively assess and articulate existing capabilities that can serve to benefit the DOD. Historical inequities in decision-making within federal agencies, including the DOD, have engrained a perception of MSIs that perpetuates an R&D landscape that lacks parity in growth opportunities. The committee focused on intervention mechanisms that target institutional planning and practices, decision-making at the DOD, facilities and administration (F&A) recuperation, and data collection on MSI capabilities.

Applying a Resource-Based Assessment to MSIs

In considering approaches to identify the assets that MSIs bring to the DOD, the committee turned to Grant's Resource-Based Theory of Competitive Advantage, a seminal theory in the field of organizational development (Barney, 1991). It emphasizes the importance of an organization's internal resources and capabilities to achieve a sustainable competitive advantage, and it posits that an organization's long-term success is grounded in its use of internal resources to contribute to higher productivity (Holdford, 2018).

Applying the five elements of contextual significance in Grant's Resource-Based Theory of Competitive Advantage may be useful to consider what different MSIs can offer to the defense research ecosystem. First is *resource heterogeneity*, in that organizations possess different types of resources and capabilities that lead to performance variations, as noted previously. Second is *resource immobility*, in which institutions have resources and organizational capabilities that may be difficult for competitors to obtain or replicate. The social complexities that contribute to the factors and characteristics of MSIs are part of that immobility. Third is the role of a *value, rarity, inimitability, and organization (VRIO) framework*. Through this framework, organizations can assess their resources and capabilities to determine their sustained competitive advantage that could result in increased R&D or cooperative agreement funding acquisition. What is most critical to this assessment framing is that an organization's rare and unreplicable resources must be organized to provide a sustainable advantage, thus implying the needs for internal systems. Fourth is the *dynamic capabilities* of an organization. Not only do organizations need to possess valuable resources, but they also need the ability to adapt, reconfigure, or renew their resource base in response to changing market conditions or competitive pressures. For MSIs this includes being able to adapt academic programming or offerings, reconfigure infrastructural operations for R&D, and be dynamic enough to respond to changes in emerging or shifting science and engineering fields. Fifth is the role of *strategic implications*. This concept emphasizes the need for an organization to focus internally on developing and leveraging its unique strengths rather than chasing external opportunities.

Addressing Potential Biases in Award Decision-Making

Efficient decision-making is an absolute necessity as it impacts an organization's ability to make choices that have the most impactful outcomes. This is particularly true in the context of the DOD. Warfighters engaged in battle must make split-second decisions to survive. A challenge for the DOD is that fast decision-making on the battlefield does not necessarily translate to the slow progression of thinking that happens in the research enterprise. The DOD program managers (PMs) must support and give institutions that are newer to its research ecosystem the time and opportunity to build a resilient infrastructure. Many non-MSIs have engaged with the DOD for decades—as is well documented—but resources at U.S. universities are unequally distributed. The top 30 institutions in R&D expenditures represent less than 3 percent of all institutions of higher education yet account for about 42 percent of the total spent on R&D expenditures (NSF, 2023).

The autonomy of PMs that allows for heuristics-based decision-making could be one causal factor that over time has led to this unequal distribution of resources. It is simply more expedient, and may seem less risky, to invest in the universities that are known performers than to seek out "startups" (i.e., universities newer to the research game). PMs could be incentivized to create diverse funding portfolios that include both the known performers (R1 universities) and the "startups" (non-R1 universities), or this could be a factor in their performance assessments. While these startups may come with greater risk, the opportunity for greater return on investment is also present. That said, when PMs add these startup universities to their portfolio, they need to acknowledge the challenges that can come with the execution of the research at the university, while recognizing the value-add in the expertise and perspective of the institution that is part of the portfolio. The PM must support and give the startup time and opportunity to build a resilient infrastructure. In addition, by having a diverse portfolio, natural mentor-mentee relationships can develop between established and startup universities to give PMs an effective yield on their investments.

Addressing Inequities in F&A Rates

The committee reviewed F&A rates, often called indirect costs (IDC), and their impact on research infrastructure growth. F&A rates are calculated based on the indirect expenditure infrastructure and support services costs incurred by an institution's direct costs. These expenditure costs are grouped into various categories, such as depreciation, utilities, libraries, and administrative expenses. When identifying F&A rates for an institution, several bases can be used, including calculating an F&A rate based on an institution's Modified Total Direct Costs (MTDC); salaries, wages, and fringe benefits; or just salaries and wages. The difference between negotiating an F&A rate based on MTDC versus salaries, wages, and fringe benefits, or just salaries and wages, lies in the cost base used to calculate and apply the F&A rate.

MTDC is the most common base used for calculating and applying F&A rates. It includes all direct salaries and wages, applicable fringe benefits, materials and supplies, services, travel, and up to the first $25,000 of each subaward (regardless of the period of performance of the subawards under the award). Notably, the MTDC rate is only available to institutions with over $10 million in yearly research expenditures. Thus, this threshold excludes many HBCUs, TCUs, and HSIs that are not R1 institutions. Alternatively, institutions may negotiate an F&A rate based on a cost base that includes only salaries, wages, and fringe benefits, or solely salaries and wages excluding fringe benefits. These F&A calculation methods result in a lower F&A calculation than MTDC, resulting in lower F&A reimbursements.

The resultant lower F&A reimbursements mean that MSIs have fewer resources to invest in building and maintaining research infrastructure, hiring administrative staff, and providing support services for researchers. With federal research funding skewing toward R1 institutions, and consequently MSIs receiving a disproportionately small share of research grants, MSIs struggle to build the necessary physical and administrative infrastructure to compete effectively for grants, creating a cyclical environment of under-investment that leads to stagnated research infrastructure growth. To rectify this self-perpetuating cycle in which MSIs struggle to compete for research funding, limiting their ability to grow their research programs and negotiate higher F&A rates, a multipronged strategy that evaluates current F&A rate negotiation policies and identifies revisions and support necessary for more equitable forward-looking IDC reimbursements must be explored.

Increasing Data Collection on MSI Capabilities

The National Academies' study *Defense Research Capacity at Historically Black Colleges and Universities and Other Minority Institutions* (NASEM, 2022) discussed the need for more data to adequately assess and monitor ongoing efforts to build research capacity and increase the DOD research dollars going to HBCUs, TCUs, and HSIs. This current study aimed to address a principal conclusion from the 2022 report: "There is insufficient data collection, inter-departmental program coordination, long-term records, and a lack of quantitative evaluations to appropriately assess" (NASEM, 2022).

The 2022 report comprehensively documented a number of data sources. One exciting departure articulated here is to initiate an effort to gather data directly from the DOD. Constructing this dataset can help in directly confronting the biases and limitations identified in the current data sources, paving the way for a more comprehensive and accurate assessment of the situation. This represents a significant step forward in the ability to measure and evaluate progress. The proposed tool would be useful as the DOD continues its efforts to build research capacity and increase the DOD research dollars going to HBCUs, HSIs, TCUs, and other MSIs. Outputs can include datasets based on queries or visual graphics such as a heat map to help decision-makers easily visualize outcomes.

RECOMMENDATIONS

Several barriers have been elucidated in this and prior studies that impact the ability of MSIs to engage meaningfully in federal R&D. These barriers often reflect the lack of resources necessary to adequately support research-engaged faculty and trainees, and facilitate ways to increase coordination of the existing research capabilities of MSIs toward equitable research partnerships that can address defense-related R&D needs. The committee explored these barriers and developed recommendations that the DOD and MSIs can implement to support the growth of research-engaged faculty and trainees and to ensure that MSIs maintain existing missions.

RECOMMENDATION 2-1: The systemic underinvestment in R&D capacity at MSIs, particularly in their infrastructure at the state and federal levels, is a pressing issue. To capture the full potential of MSIs, it is imperative that the DOD, with congressional support, introduce mechanisms for dedicated funding for non-R1 MSIs to foster research infrastructure growth including funding facilities and equipment. Potential forms of support could include the following:

- Providing direct support for investment in facilities and equipment to increase R&D relevant to national needs for MSIs such as TCUs, which span multiple states, and private HBCUs, which receive less state support than their public counterparts.
- Providing matching funds for states to invest in research infrastructure growth at MSIs seeking to increase their research infrastructure. These matching funds will incentivize state and local governments that have fallen short of authorizations, which has led to systemic and inequitable underinvestment in MSIs.

RECOMMENDATION 3-1: For MSIs to contribute more fully to defense-related research, research capacity and talent must be developed and strengthened. This is a unique strategic opportunity for the DOD and national security. Many MSIs (in particular TCUs) embody distinctive perspectives and so have the potential to make completely unique research contributions in areas such as addressing agricultural systems that are resilient in drought conditions. These distinctive ways of thinking, problem-solving, and social organization should be of interest to both the DOD and the broader scientific community. Investing in investigators at non-R1 MSIs will not only increase the defense-related research capacity base nationally, but also deepen and diversify the available investigators that can support and advance the Department's R&D needs.

- To partially engage this opportunity, the DOD, with support from Congress, should develop and administer a DOD MSI Investigator Award for very capable scholars at HBCUs, TCUs, and MSIs. This new program should be modeled after existing department programs such as the DARPA Young Faculty Award, Air Force Young Investigator Program, and ONR Young Investigator Program. In the implementation of DOD MSI Investigator awards, the following factors should be included:

- Up to 100 awards made per year across the Department's branches (Air Force, Navy, Army, etc.).
- Tracking of the number of awards made to each institution type to guide evaluation, outreach, and programmatic planning.
- An average of $150,000 per grant per year over a 5-year grant period with the option to renew. This sustained funding will include funding that enables each DOD MSI Investigator to establish a research lab at their institution, pursue topics relevant to the DOD's R&D needs, and serve as a focal point for increased engagement for defense-related research.
- Cohorts of investigators should be convened in-person on an annual basis to discuss successes, roadblocks, and recommendations to refine and reshape this program based on the unique and not-well-understood challenges and opportunities at their sites with the identification appropriate metrics for evaluation.
- The focus should be on faculty at HBCUs, TCUs, and non-R1 MSIs with award recipients providing 51 percent of their effort to the funded research project during the duration of the award. The National Institutes of Health PIONEER award and Howard Hughes Medical Institute Program may serve as models for an agency-wide program that supports promising scientists across career stages in addressing high-risk/high-reward issues relevant to the DOD's mission.
- The DOD should avoid the use of 'tenure track" designated faculty as a criterion. The use of "tenure track" appointments creates a barrier for engagement for smaller institutions such as TCUs. As a result, any program focused on developing researchers at non-R1 MSIs that use "tenure track" as an eligibility criterion would preclude both their engagement from these institutions and the DOD from broadening its potential researcher base.
- Review criteria and processes should be developed with an advisory council that includes researchers and research administrators from MSIs and institutions with historical engagement with the DOD.

RECOMMENDATION 3-2: To support the existing missions of MSIs to educate and provide support for investigator release time, the DOD should develop a postdoctoral fellowship program for MSIs geared toward doctoral recipients with specialized expertise in defense-related research areas, broad disciplinary understanding, and interest in developing instructional skills. Funding that provides relief for course and research support at MSIs will help incentivize institutions where teaching loads prohibit significant engagement in research. It can also help support the careers of postdocs pursuing experience as faculty. The DOD should incorporate the following into the program:

- Recipients can allot 50 percent of their time as a research associate within the lab of a faculty member conducting defense-related research and 50 percent of their time to teach courses typically covered by the investigator.
- The duration of the fellowship should correspond with the length of a typical research grant to ensure continuity in course coverage. It should be affixed to non-R1 primary teaching institutions and DOD-relevant MSI funding mechanisms.
- A matching mechanism that connects prospective fellows with MSI faculty should facilitate awarded fellows' identification of a supervising investigator.
- A postdoctoral mentoring plan should be included. Mentoring plans should be standardized to ensure continuity in support for fellows, and mentors should receive training on mentorship.

RECOMMENDATION 3-3: Inter-institutional collaborations among MSIs are an underutilized strategy to leverage unique perspectives, skills, and abilities to further the DOD research objectives. Frequently, no single institution possesses the necessary breadth of talent to broadly serve the DOD's research needs. Furthermore, under-resourced administrative staff often disincentivize MSI collaborations, especially when a well-resourced Primarily White Institutions R1 is poised to take the lead. To increase capacity development and engagement, the DOD should develop a funding program to support the creation of research consortia with an HBCU, TCU, HSI or other non-R1 MSI lead. The research consortia would focus on a clear area or project and include scholars from three or more MSIs. The committee is aware of the Research Institute for Tactical Autonomy, led by Howard University, an HBCU, and recommends that additional consortia be developed to address research projects of critical need to the DOD to facilitate the engagement of more MSIs. In the implementation of this funding program, the following factors should be included:

- Support for developing consortia that fund R&D.
- Funding for at least 5 years for each consortium to support planning, execution, and evaluation activities.
- Support for consortia that exhibit intentional and equitable collaboration and mutually beneficial partnerships through strategies, including at least 6 months of pre-award communication, partnership agreements, and/or articulated resource and personnel sharing frameworks.
- Planning grants for prospective consortia to develop full proposals.
- Supplements for institutional mentorship between MSIs and known performers to assist with the consortia's planning and implementation.

RECOMMENDATION 3-4: An under-resourced administrative infrastructure to secure, manage, and coordinate grants, contracts, and other opportunities is a significant barrier to engagement in the DOD and other federal agency opportunities. To increase the ability of under-resourced MSIs to adequately and effectively participate in opportunities, the DOD, with congressional support, should develop a funding program to develop administrative hubs. The administrative hubs would allow MSIs the option to coordinate through a professional organization that possesses the administrative expertise and resources necessary to support grant and contract acquisition and management (pre- and post-award). The hubs could also coordinate faculty and student participation in DOD opportunities, and communicate the current and evolving capabilities of member institutions. Additionally, these hubs would be used by three or more non-R1 MSIs that are regionally located or geographically close to facilitate coordination and mutual use and complications due to differences in administrative policies, complexities and protocols need to be built into use agreements. In the implementation of this program, the following factors should be included:
- Funding for at least 5 years to launch each hub and facilitate planning, execution, and evaluation.
- Support for lead organizations with clearly articulated missions relevant to MSIs who exhibit intentional development through strategies, such as the following:
  - Referencing at least 6 months of pre-award communication,
  - Partnership agreements with participating institutions,
  - An administrative capability track record, and

- o Clearly defined sustainability plans that demonstrate maintenance and long-term administrative support for participating institutions post-award.
- Planning grants for prospective hubs to develop full proposals.

To better coordinate this engagement DOD-wide and track and increase success toward more engagement, the committee proposes several strategies for evaluation and coordination that provide interagency coordination and sharing of best practices. A significant impediment to engagement with DOD R&D is a lack of awareness of the diversity of R&D supported by the Department. When exploring the DOD's Critical Technology Areas (CTAs) and dissecting the components of each CTA, the committee found that most MSIs possess academic programs equivalent to one or more of the CTAs. To better engage with DOD R&D, the Department, Congress, and MSIs must conduct a thorough evaluation that matches current programs at MSIs to the basic and applied components of the CTAs. Exploring these areas through internal and external engagement pathways could leverage existing infrastructure, increase the efficacy of outreach activities, and identify a more comprehensive view of R&D that is inclusive across disciplines to increase engagement and advance the DOD's research and workforce needs.

RECOMMENDATION 4-1: Engaging the breadth of research disciplines relevant to national security is necessary to fully explore opportunities and increase MSIs' engagement in defense-related R&D. Congress should create programs that increase the utilization of the full breadth of the DOD's research in non-engineering disciplines.

- **The DOD should further develop its research capacity by including and expanding funding to support the social sciences in its calls for proposals, focusing on the unique perspective MSIs bring to these fields. HBCUs, TCUs, and MSIs can provide rich contributions in the social sciences and other non-engineering-focused disciplines that are critical to DOD research.**

RECOMMENDATION 4-2: Beginning in FY2026,[2] the DOD Under Secretary of Defense for Research and Engineering should collect and

---

[2] This text was updated after release of the report to the study sponsor to reflect the fiscal year for the DOD to implement changes.

publish data annually that measure the efficacy of existing outreach programs targeting MSIs, and share lessons learned with DOD agencies to accelerate the dissemination of best practices.

- This report should include a longitudinal analysis to provide evidence of successful engagement and impact. Potential metrics should include the following:
  - Number of MSIs engaged quarterly,
  - Data on personnel interacted with (investigators, administrators, students),
  - Institution type,
  - Hours and type of engagement,
  - Number of applications received and time to successful award, and
  - Measurement of research infrastructure growth among awardees (instrumentation, research-engaged faculty, administration support, etc.).
- Metrics collected should be used to set a baseline for improvement of how the DOD engages with MSIs. They should be assessed annually to direct resources and engagement activities toward increased participation in DOD R&D.
- The DOD Under Secretary of Defense for Research and Engineering should administer new outreach programs that do the following:
  - Create and deploy a DOD liaison to HBCUs, TCUs, and MSIs to translate the DOD's interests to the university and university capabilities and interests to the DOD.
  - Place scientists and engineers from local military labs at MSIs to teach STEM courses and provide course load relief for investigators pursuing and conducting defense-related research, as referenced in Chapter 3. A potential framework could be the use of the Intergovernmental Personnel Act Mobility Program.[3]
  - The DOD Under Secretary of Defense for Research and Engineering should expand existing outreach programs so that HBCU, TCU, and MSI employees are eligible for sabbaticals to gain R&D experience with DOD acquisition and operations organizations.

---

[3] For more information, see https://www.doi.gov/pmb/hr/ipa-mobility-program.

These new outreach programs will allow for increased awareness and provide teaching load relief to HBCU, TCU, and MSI faculty conducting DOD R&D. In doing so, however, DOD's HBCU/MI programs should address institutions' unique contexts and needs rather than group HBCU, TCU, HSI, and other MSI engagements. A one-size-fits-all approach decreases the successful engagement of MSIs, given the diversity of needs, challenges, engagement, and opportunities within and across MSIs. To plan and implement more granular interventions, the DOD should undertake robust comment periods, listening sessions, and dialogue with institutions and their supporting communities to develop engagement frameworks tailored to each MSI type to increase the Department's success in its engagement with MSIs and relationship development activities. This approach is both in the strategic interest of the DOD and helps support global competitiveness, national security, and historic disparities.

RECOMMENDATION 4-3: The DOD should allocate resources to assess the potential for regional connectivity and partnerships between existing DOD labs, UARCs, and FFRDCs, and local or regional HBCUs, TCUs, and MSIs. This assessment should include collecting metrics on existing and potential research collaborations between these entities.

- Based on this assessment described above, the DOD should provide guidance to DOD labs, UARCs, and FFRDCs about how to support and expand collaborative R&D with MSIs within proximity or sharing similar research foci.
- The DOD should develop a pilot funding opportunity that allows MSI investigators to develop research projects with investigators at DOD labs, UARCs, and FFRDCs. Awards should include MSI investigators as lead investigators, co-investigators, or lead contractors.

RECOMMENDATION 4-4: The DOD Under Secretary of Defense for Research and Engineering should create programs for evaluating and assessing MSI institutional capacity building. Specifically, this would include a program that supports the development of a "lessons learned" report on building, operating, and maintaining lab infrastructure to conduct unclassified R&D at MSIs. Special considerations should also be given to the unique ability of many MSIs, such as TCUs, to conduct classified research and to the strategic advantage of geographic locations like institutions that are remote. These additional funds should be aimed at understanding and communicating information relevant to long-term capacity building at MSIs. Information that could be examined in such a report might include best practices for the following:

- Standardizing and accelerating institutional R&D capability with a focus on physical plant and equipment investments;
- Increasing the institutional success rate;
- Identifying strategies for developing partnerships with non-R1 MSIs; and
- Identifying approaches by institution type (HBCU, TCU, non-R1 MSI), highest degree offered, level of research engagement, and geography.

RECOMMENDATION 5-1: MSIs that seek to increase their R&D footprint, elevate across Carnegie Classifications, and/or improve the rate at which they secure funding should develop an internal strategic plan that advances their R&D goals and clearly articulates their unique value. Such plans could include the following elements:

- Principles of the Resource-Based Theory of Competitive Advantage.
- An institutional SWOT (Strengths, Weaknesses, Opportunities, Threats) analysis or other strategic analysis to identify specific areas of the DOD's interest in which its capabilities could have outsized impact.
- A 10-year roadmap to guide and prioritize internal investments and engagement with relevant DOD sponsors. Investments could include infrastructure, instrumentation, personnel, curriculum, and/or services.
- For institutions with demonstrated need, the DOD and other federal agencies should provide grants for institutional assessment and strategic planning toward increased research engagement and capacity building.

RECOMMENDATION 5-2: The DOD should intentionally engage MSIs as part of its R&D portfolio to competitively seek the broadest range of ideas and innovators possible. Increasing the diversity of institutions and researchers actively engaged in the DOD's research ecosystem will support increased global competition, undergird national security, and increase innovations that protect the warfighter. In implementing this increased engagement, the following factors should be included:

- Metrics on the number of current and new grant awards and contracting programs to institutions of higher education, with coding to identify MSIs by type, on an annual basis beginning in FY2026. Data should also capture dollar amounts for each award to establish a baseline for growth that dates back to FY2011.
- A tangible goal, set annually by the Office of the Under Secretary of Defense for Research and Engineering, for growing the awards and contracts granted to MSIs as the lead applicants for funding opportunities for each program.
- An assessment by the Office of the Under Secretary of Defense for Research and Engineering of MSI success rates and program performer diversity at the end of each fiscal year. This metric can address the DOD's needs by capturing MSI engagement and project relevance to the Department's mission as data for goal-setting in subsequent fiscal years.
- The introduction of training on best practices and implicit bias. The incorporation of best practices and training to address implicit bias in the grant-making process will equip PMs with tools to ensure assessments of institutions and funding decisions are devoid of any implicit biases that may impact proposals from previously under engaged institutions.

RECOMMENDATION 5-3: To support the growth and development of research programs at MSIs, Congress should provide dedicated funding to help HBCUs, TCUs, and non-R1 HSIs build and maintain state-of-the-art research facilities and equipment. This investment will enable MSIs to compete more effectively for research grants. An example of a program that can be adapted is the 1890 Facilities Grant Program. A similar funding mechanism will provide support for the development and improvement of facilities, equipment, and libraries necessary to conduct defense-related research.

- Congress should also evaluate the effectiveness of the existing F&A de minimis rate[4] and set a de minimis rate that does the following:

---

[4] The de minimis IDC rate is 10 percent of an organization's MTDC: 2 CFR 200.414.

     ○ **Allows for institutions seeking to increase R&D activity to receive a more adequate reimbursement for engagement in federally funded R&D.**

     ○ **Is higher for smaller institutions to support increased engagement in federally funded R&D.**

- **Additionally, federal agencies should implement an F&A Cost Rate Support Project to provide ongoing technical assistance and support to MSIs in developing and negotiating their F&A rates. The basis of F&A rates for MSIs should be different than for other institutions because institutions with historic investments by states and the federal government benefit from the current structure while MSIs continue to suffer current inequities that are a direct consequence of prior investment disparities in research-focused facilities, equipment, and infrastructure. This will help ensure these historically disadvantaged institutions receive more appropriate F&A reimbursements for their research activities and increase their ability to contribute to U.S. R&D, global competition, and national security.**

A PLAN FOR INCREASED ENGAGEMENT IN DOD R&D

The study committee's charge was to conduct an assessment of the activities necessary to increase the engagement of MSIs in defense-related research, where possible elevate to R1 status, and identify strategies for tracking and increasing the capacity of MSIs to address the R&D needs of the DOD. The committee recognizes these efforts take time and resources on the part of the DOD and institutions. However, when collected and used, the recommendations can help the DOD more effectively assess its current and ongoing impact and better plan its future interventions. To better understand how MSIs can increase their capacity for R&D, it is essential to identify and address the barriers that have historically impacted their engagement. Many MSIs were developed as teaching institutions, providing the only opportunity for members of the communities they serve to receive an education. Those missions have persisted through times of underfunding and historic marginalization. Regardless of the underinvestment and historic missions, MSIs have continued to grow the breadth and scope of their academic offerings and research capacity. Furthermore, HBCUs, TCUs, HSIs, and other MSIs provide a diversity of perspectives that will support innovation and advancements that will improve the nation's competitiveness and national security. To facilitate this innovation and engage these institutions fully, Congress, the DOD, and other federal agencies must address existing barriers, explore unique strategies, and develop frameworks that allow MSIs to grow their capabilities and retain their uniqueness with intentionality that supports the assets that they have always possessed.

REFERENCES

Barney, J. 1991. Firm resources and sustained competitive advantage. *Journal of Management,* *17*(1), 99-120.

Holdford, D.A. 2018. Resource-based theory of competitive advantage—a framework for pharmacy practice innovation research. *Pharmacy Practice* (Granada), *16*(3).

NASEM (National Academies of Sciences, Engineering, and Medicine). 2019. *Minority serving institutions: America's underutilized resource for strengthening the STEM workforce.* Washington, DC: The National Academies Press. https://doi.org/10.17226/25257.

NASEM. 2020. *Evaluation of the Minerva Research Initiative.* Washington, DC: The National Academies Press. https://doi.org/10.17226/25482.

NASEM. 2022. *Defense research capacity at historically black colleges and universities and other minority institutions: Transitioning from good intentions to measurable outcomes.* Washington, DC: The National Academies Press. https://doi.org/10.17226/26399.

NASEM. 2024. *Building defense research capacity at historically black colleges and universities, tribal colleges and universities, and minority-serving institutions: Proceedings of three town halls.* Washington, DC: The National Academies Press. https://doi.org/10.17226/27511.

NSF (National Science Foundation). 2023. R&D expenditures at U.S. universities increased by $8 billion in FY 2022. National Center for Science and Engineering Statistics. https://ncses.nsf.gov/pubs/nsf24307.

U.S. Census. 2018. Demographic turning points for the United States: Population projections for 2020 to 2060. https://www.census.gov/content/dam/Census/library/publications/2020/demo/p25-1144.pdf.

1

Introduction

The research and development (R&D) landscape in the United States, including previously sponsored Department of Defense (DOD) R&D, has profoundly impacted the lives of Americans and the nation's systems of health, innovation, and security domestically and globally. The R&D ecosystem has precipitated new therapeutics, advancements in energy production, industries, and the science and technology necessary to protect the nation's defense and security, including dual use technologies. Many lifesaving advancements are considered "dual use technology." For example, the same satellite imagery exploitation software used to find strategic missile threats is used to find cancerous cells in women's breasts. Since World War II, DOD and other federal agencies have been instrumental in supporting the R&D of the dual-use technologies that have been precipitates of the U.S. R&D ecosystem (NRC, 1994). For these capabilities to continue to advance, it is increasingly important that the full breadth of the nation's R&D capacity is prepared and engaged to support its current and future needs. Minority-serving institutions (MSIs) provide a channel through which the DOD investments in R&D capacity can develop new strategic alliances, find new talent, and drive technology to compete against global adversaries.

In 2022, the National Academies of Sciences, Engineering, and Medicine (the National Academies) released a consensus study entitled *Defense Research Capacity at Historically Black Colleges and Universities and Other Minority Institutions: Transitioning from Good Intentions to Measurable*

Outcomes (NASEM, 2022). The report provided overarching conclusions and recommendations on how the DOD and Congress can increase the engagement of historically underfunded and underrecognized communities and institutions in national security. The recommendations include increased appropriations, long-term institutional support, better data tracking and metrics gathering, and learning from other federal agencies on best practices to fully engage Historically Black Colleges and Universities (HBCUs), Tribal Colleges and Universities (TCUs), Hispanic-Serving Institutions (HSIs), and other MSIs. The study committee developed two frameworks for agencies and institutions to understand (1) the elements of institutional capacity to procure and administer DOD-related research, and (2) the spectrum of research activity across MSIs. These frameworks were designed to help the DOD and institutions assess where within the research spectrum a given institution exists and what variables are necessary to strengthen its research experience, productivity, and capacity.

This current report responds to a request from the DOD for strategies to build on these frameworks and recommendations so that the DOD, Congress, institutions, and other stakeholders can move forward.

IMPORTANCE AND TIMELINESS OF STUDY

Competition among nations provides an incentive for increased support for science, technology, engineering, and mathematics (STEM). Success in this competition includes targeted investments in R&D that support innovation and education of a STEM-ready workforce (Mazarr et al., 2018). While the United States remains a leader globally, several countries have increased their STEM investments with the goal of supplanting U.S. standing. The impact is exacerbated by competition with countries that have taken an aggressive posture with the United States. In this environment, national security runs the risk of becoming compromised if investments in STEM are not only maintained but increased to safeguard the nation's status amidst this competition. In recent years, countries such as China have operationalized ambitious policies to increase their highly skilled STEM workforce, expanding the number of citizens who are able to engage in their STEM enterprise and support their national defense. It is estimated that by 2025, excluding international graduates, China will produce three times more STEM PhDs than the United States (Zwetsloot et al., 2021). To continue a homogeneous path will yield the same results and the country runs the risk of falling behind its adversaries, with national security and defense becoming vulnerable. Alternately, cognitively diverse perspectives in R&D can help with problem-solving, innovation, and out-of-the-box thinking when challenges rise.

To address historical inequities and the importance of increasing access and engagement of underserved communities in the U.S. STEM ecosystem, the White House released a national vision for "STEMM Equity and Excellence" in late 2022 (White House Office of Science & Technology Policy, 2022). The vision statement calls for the federal government to work to dismantle barriers of access that contribute to the historical under-investment in underrepresented communities and that impact American global competitiveness. Congress and federal agencies have underscored this need by developing programs and introducing legislation with the goal of increasing the U.S. R&D performer base, specifically targeting MSIs as conduits for increasing the diversity of institutions and individuals that support the U.S. STEM enterprise. Since 1987, the National Defense Authorization Acts (NDAAs) have directed the DOD to establish programs and policies that support capacity building at MSIs, recognizing that more needs to be done to systematically increase engagement and participation in defense-related R&D.

In response to H.R. 7900–NDAA for FY23 Sec. 233 (Appendix C) and the NDAA for FY20 Sec. 220,[1] the DOD approached the National Academies to identify tangible frameworks for increasing the participation of MSIs in defense-related R&D and, where possible, identify the necessary mechanisms for elevating some MSIs to R1 status (doctoral universities with very high research activity) on the Carnegie Classification of Institutions of Higher Education scale.[2] Research activity at MSIs does add to the body of knowledge. Whether at primarily undergraduate or graduate-degree institutions, it also contributes to the education of talent in STEM and other fields. As students work in research activities in laboratories, in archives, or with complex datasets, they learn their disciplines in depth and ready themselves to serve the nation. Research can be an essential dimension of education at the college level or in advanced study, whether at TCUs, HBCUs, or HSIs. It must be noted that research in U.S. higher education is not only the province of Carnegie R1 institutions. Primarily undergraduate

---

[1] Text - H.R.7776 - 117th Congress (2021-2022): James M. Inhofe National Defense Authorization Act for Fiscal Year 2023. (2022, December 23). https://www.congress.gov/bill/117th-congress/house-bill/7776/text.

[2] For more information on the Carnegie Classification of Institutions of Higher Education, see https://carnegieclassifications.acenet.edu/.

institutions contribute significantly to knowledge formation, not only in the sciences but also in domains such as area studies or international affairs. The examples are many. Graduates of these institutions go on to advance study at many august U.S. graduate programs. The nation needs to promote the pipeline of domestic students to these programs. Our MSIs are an important and needed source. To address this charge, the National Academies appointed a committee to do the following:

1. Summarize previous National Academies' reports on MSIs, including capacity development and engagement in U.S. R&D;
2. Assess the activities and investments necessary to, where possible, elevate additional MSIs to R1 status and increase their participation in defense-related R&D and industries; and
3. Identify goals, incentives, and metrics to measure MSI capacity to address the DOD's needs in engineering, research, and development.

The committee's full statement of task can be found in Box 1-1, and the biographical sketches of the committee members in Appendix B.

In 2022, the DOD also released an Equity Action Plan that operationalizes President Biden's Executive Order 13985, Advancing Racial Equity and Support for Underserved Communities Through the Federal Government. Included in the plan was a commitment to establish a department-wide approach to "invest in under-served communities and expand access to the DOD programs and opportunities by increasing investments in minority-serving institutions (MSIs) and investments in K-12 and K-20 programs" (U.S. Department of Defense, 2022). These investments include refining outreach and partnerships; facilitating more MSI-centered events; and increasing MSI access to internships, grants, scholarships, and R&D opportunities. Through a targeted approach that ensures that all U.S. academic institutions and the communities they serve are engaged in R&D opportunities, the DOD (and the federal government as a whole) will be able to diversify and expand the nation's research performer base and propel its dominance into the future.

Many strategies outlined in the DOD's Equity Action Plan align with the National Academies' 2022 report and recommendations. However, proper frameworks and implementation of the full scope of the various recommendations have not yet been executed, leaving a large portion of the U.S. R&D enterprise underutilized. The current study provides

BOX 1-1
Statement of Task

An ad hoc committee of the National Academies of Sciences, Engineering, and Medicine will examine defense-related STEM activities at HBCUs, TCUs, HSIs, and other minority-serving institutions, with a primary focus on engineering and research and development activities and provide recommendations that identify 1) actions that may be taken by the Secretary of Defense, Congress, HBCUs, TCUs, HSIs, and other minority-serving institutions, and other agencies or organizations to increase the participation of HBCUs, TCUs, HSIs, and other minority-serving institutions in defense-related research activities, and 2) a set of specific goals, incentives, and metrics to increase and measure the capacity of HBCUs, TCUs, HSIs, and other minority-serving institutions to address DOD's engineering and research and development needs.

The study includes the following:

1. Summaries of the assessments provided in previous related National Academies reports, including assessments of:
   a. the engineering and research and development capabilities of HBCUs, TCUs, HSIs, and other minority-serving institutions, including the workforce and physical research infrastructure;
   b. the ability of HBCUs, TCUs, HSIs, and other minority-serving institutions to participate in defense-related engineering and research and development activities; and
   c. the ability of HBCUs, TCUs, HSIs, and other minority-serving institutions to compete effectively for defense-related engineering and research and development contracts.
2. An assessment of the activities and investments necessary:
   a. to elevate HBCUs, TCUs, HSIs, and other minority-serving institutions to R1 status on the Carnegie Classification of Institutions of Higher Education;
   b. to increase the participation of HBCUs, TCUs, HSIs, and other minority-serving institutions in defense-related engineering and research and development activities;
   c. to expand the support provided by the DOD and defense-related industries to HBCUs, TCUs, HSIs, and other minority-serving institutions to include the

continued

BOX 1-1 Continued

development or enhancement of grant and contract administration capabilities; and

d. to increase the ability of such institutions to effectively compete for defense-related engineering and research and development contracts (HBCU/TCU/HSI/etc. targeted and open funding opportunities) through the identification of the necessary infrastructure to carry out research in subject areas deemed in-demand by the DOD.

3. A set of specific goals, incentives, and metrics to increase and measure the capacity of HBCUs, TCUs, HSIs, and other minority-serving institutions to address the engineering, research, and development needs of the DOD, including:

a. Strategies for the provision of long-term institutional support to HBCUs, TCUs, HSIs, and other minority-serving institutions including an assessment of DOD staffing dedicated to engagement with HBCUs, TCUs, HSIs, and other minority-serving institutions, the development and enhancement of the physical research infrastructure and research activities at HBCUs, TCUs, HSIs, and other minority-serving institutions, and the expansion of grant and contract administration capabilities of HBCUs, TCUs, HSIs, and other minority-serving institutions

b. Methods to strengthen support for HBCUs, TCUs, HSIs, and other minority-serving institutions within and across military departments and other organizations, including the identification of new grant solicitation evaluation options

c. Plans to improve data collection with respect to HBCUs, TCUs, HSIs, and other minority-serving institutions applying for and/or receiving support from the DOD and other federal agencies

recommendations of strategies that the DOD, Congress, and other relevant communities can implement to increase the engagement of MSIs in R&D.

CHANGING DEMOGRAPHICS AND MSIs

Engaging the full breadth of talent in the United States is an important component of growing and sustaining dominance in R&D and supporting national security into the future. By 2030, one-fifth of Americans will be above age 65 and at or nearing retirement from the workforce. Looking further out, the United States will see huge shifts in the diversity and composition of its population in the next 50 years. While projections indicate overall, albeit slowing, growth in the total U.S. population, the demographic composition is anticipated to be vastly different in succeeding generations. Estimates of race and ethnic demographic changes between 2016 and 2030 show a decrease in the non-Hispanic white population and an increase in terms of both number and share of all other demographic groups (U.S. Census, 2018). These population shifts signal a citizenry and workforce that will be increasingly diverse and require targeted support to ensure the country's population has the resources to engage meaningfully in the needs of the nation.

In order to capitalize on changing demographics, investment in DOD research at MSIs provides a unique opportunity to focus efforts on engaging the changing U.S. population. Consider the following:

- HBCUs enroll 9 percent of all Black/African American students pursuing degrees in higher education (NCES, 2022). While small in comparison to the number of Black/African American students across all academic institutions, HBCUs have an oversized impact on Black/African American students pursing degrees in fields relevant to the DOD's R&D. In fact, 25 percent of Black/African American students who are awarded degrees in STEM received those degrees at an HBCU (White House, 2021).
- In the 2015-2016 academic year, 11.7 percent of all American Indian/Alaska Native students attended a TCU. While overall enrollment of American Indian and Alaska Native students has decreased across higher education, there is significant growth in the number of Indigenous students attending TCUs (Marroquín, 2019).

- HSIs enroll 63 percent of all Hispanic/Latinx students. The populations at these institutions are expected to grow, as is the total number of institutions that can be classified as an HSI based on the percent threshold of Hispanic/Latinx students (Excelencia in Education, 2024).
- The subgroups of High Hispanic Enrollment (HHE) and High American Indian and Alaska Native Enrolling (HAIANE) institutions provide a significant opportunity to focus support for increased impact.

These data reflect the overall enrollment of underrepresented communities in higher education. Furthermore, the ability of MSIs not only to educate underrepresented individuals but also to nurture high achievement throughout learners' lifetimes solidifies the critical role these institutions play in the U.S. higher education landscape and the DOD's mission and priorities. Between 2010 and 2020, doctoral recipients who identify as a racial minority such as Black/African American, Hispanic/Latinx, or Alaska Native or Native American disproportionately received their baccalaureate degrees from Minority Institutions/MSIs (Einaudi et al., 2022). HBCUs accounted for 25.7 percent of Black individuals who received their doctorate; HHEs produced 42.4 percent of Hispanic and Latinx students who received their doctorate; and TCUs/HAIANEs and HHEs produced 26 percent of all American Indian and Alaska Native doctoral recipients. The aforementioned institutions disproportionately educate underrepresented and underutilized communities and provide an essential leveraging point for increasing the engagement of said communities. The impacts of the instruction and environment at MSIs have a multiplying effect on the outcomes of underrepresented communities. This provides an opportunity for the DOD and other federal agencies seeking to increase investments and participation of the communities they serve to target their efforts to support growth in MSI capacity. MSIs are well positioned to educate and conduct research that increases the skill sets learned by their students and to provide federal agencies with a way to meaningfully engage with a future workforce. While programs targeting increased engagement of MSIs have been in existence, little momentum has been demonstrated to date that exhibits how prior investments have achieved more engagement of under-resourced and underutilized MSIs. This report seeks to identify novel strategies that both leverage existing infrastructure and programs for institutions of higher education and propose new programs and policies to effectively increase engagement.

COMMITTEE APPROACH

To address its statement of task, the committee held nine committee meetings and five open sessions. The open sessions were used to investigate existing MSI engagement strategies across the DOD branches and R&D programs, as well as learn about opportunities for collaboration and support with University Affiliated Research Centers and Federally Funded Research and Development Centers. The committee also invited speakers from other federal agency programs involved in data collection or addressing the various components of capacity development at emerging research institutions to understand their frameworks and funding structures and elucidate best practices to identify mechanisms that could be adapted for the DOD. The committee also received a briefing from the American Council on Education on the forthcoming changes to the Carnegie Classification of Institutions of Higher Education to better understand the metrics that will inform the revision.

The committee conducted three site visits to receive candid feedback and develop an assessment of institutional capacity and opportunities. The site visits represented three targeted institution types (HBCU, TCU, and HSI) and included Fayetteville State University, Diné College, and California State University at Bakersfield that are engaged in research but are below R2 (High Research Activity) on the Carnegie Classification of Institutions of Higher Education scale to identify potential interventions for increasing capacity at these diverse and often under-supported institutions. Recognizing that each school is unique, and these schools do not capture all HBCUs, TCUs, or HSIs, such as MSIs with engineering departments, the visits were invaluable to expose committee members to the on-the-ground experiences of leaders, administrators, faculty, and students, as well as to tour facilities and other infrastructure.

The committee also developed and distributed a Request for Information (RFI) publicly available through the National Academies' website and other channels. The goals of the RFI were to collect information on how MSIs broadly assess their current research, resources, and capabilities; determine their research aspirations in defense-related research and industries critical to U.S. national security; and learn how they currently engage with the DOD.

A commissioned paper by Ruishan Zhang drew on National Science Foundation data to characterize current research capacity and explore potential investment avenues.[3]

---

[3] The paper is available at https://nap.nationalacademies.org/catalog/27838.

The committee drew on the proceedings of a series of Town Halls, sponsored by the DOD and convened by the National Academies through a separate committee in 2023 (NASEM, 2024). The Town Halls provided a rich array of perspectives from the government, institutions, nonprofits, and other organizations.

Finally, as requested in the statement of task, the committee reviewed previous National Academies' studies (listed in Chapter 2) and relevant literature. Points drawn from the site visits, RFI, commissioned paper, Town Halls, and other inputs are highlighted throughout this report and contributed to the committee's final recommendations and suggestions.

DEFINITIONS AND SCOPE

Research Capacity

The previous National Academies' report (NASEM, 2022, p. 4) provided a framework to consider what research capacity entails. Because it is so critical to the current study, it is useful to refer to it here. That committee identified three mutually enforcing areas:

1. A strong institutional grant and contract base, including appropriate physical research facilities and skilled research support to enable competitiveness.
2. Research faculty support, including an articulated vision and support for a research climate and culture by institutional leadership, faculty teaching workloads that allow time for research pursuits, and department/college-based research and administrative staff.
3. Ancillary services, including effective human resources processes, legal/contracting assistance, and robust government relations teams.

Minority-Serving Institutions

Minority Institutions (MI) are institutions of higher education whose enrollment of a single minority or a combination of minorities exceeds 50 percent of the total enrollment as defined by §365(3) of the Higher Education Act. MSIs are institutions of higher education enrolling populations with significant percentages of undergraduate minority students, or that serve certain populations of minority students, and may have been historically founded by mission to serve the population enrolled (Box 1-2).

BOX 1-2
Minority Institutions and Minority-Serving Institutions

Minority Institutions (MIs) are institutions of higher education whose enrollment of a single minority or a combination of minorities exceeds 50 percent of the total enrollment as defined by §365(3) of the Higher Education Act.

Minority-Serving Institutions (MSIs) are institutions of higher education enrolling populations with significant percentages of undergraduate minority students, or that serve certain populations of minority students, and may have been historically founded by mission to serve the population enrolled.

The committee's premise to use MSI recognizes the mission-centeredness to serve a specific population of minorities versus the classification based on contemporary enrollment trends for populations of minority students in MIs.

Institutions that serve primarily minority populations are identified in law, policy discourse, and even in National Academies' reports specifically as "minority institutions" or "minority-serving institutions." After recognition of the different ways in which institutions were formed and currently operate, the committee drew from its statement of task to consistently use the term "minority-serving institution" or MSI throughout this report, unless quoting from a source that used "minority institution" or MI. Further discussion can be found in Chapter 2.[4]

Another decision point centered on MSI research expenditures. Several MSIs are potentially eligible to be elevated to R1 (very high research activity) on the reformed Carnegie Classification of Institutions of Higher Education proposed for 2025 due to increased expenditures and increased diversity of conferred research doctoral degrees being offered. The

---

[4] As defined in U.S. federal statute (20 U.S. Code § 1067k), a "minority institution" (MI) is a specific term referring to an institution of higher education whose enrollment of a single minority or a combination of minorities exceeds 50 percent of the total enrollment. This contrasts with the term "minority-serving institution," which federal statute (20 U.S. Code § 1067q) defines as "institutions that range in enrollment from 10-40 percent of a single minority group."

committee looked at recent expenditures reported in the Higher Education Research and Development (HERD) Survey conducted by the National Science Foundation and divided institutions by percentile. As has been reported in previous studies, the top one-third of institutions account for the majority of higher education R&D expenditures. By and large, most MSIs fall below the 66th percentile of institutions that report their expenditures on the HERD Survey (Zhang, 2024). For this reason, the committee chose to focus its recommendations and findings on MSIs that report less than $200 million in federal expenditures annually in the HERD Survey. This delineation was selected to support non-R1 MSIs as well as to ensure that any interventions provided by Congress, the DOD, or other federal agencies support MSIs that are newly minted R1 institutions and that require support to sustain their classification.

Defense-Related Research

To address its statement of task, the committee sought to define defense-related research that could be broadly applied and provide an opportunity to contextualize better the capabilities of MSIs. The committee chose to use STEM throughout the study in its assessment and recommendations. The acronym "STEM" used in this report includes disciplines that are traditionally described when referring to "STEM," namely, science, technology, engineering, and mathematics. Additionally, given the DOD's interest in biomedical research, the committee also chose to incorporate medicine when the report references "STEM" disciplines. While most defense-related research is funded and conducted through the DOD and its related industries, defense-related research permeates the breadth and scope of science, engineering, and medicine, and funding and support for defense-related research and infrastructure exists across the federal government. Agencies such as the National Science Foundation, National Institutes of Health, National Aeronautics and Space Administration, Department of Energy, and others all include programs and funding supporting defense-related research. Thus, the committee developed the following definition:

> Defense-related research is basic, applied, or experimental research encompassing advancing scientific discovery, technological development, prototypes, and operational systems or digital technologies that contribute to the DOD mission priorities to (1) defend the nation through innovation and modernization,

(2) protect the people through human-centered technological advances such as psychological and medical advances, and (3) promote success through teamwork that includes strengthening partnerships to respond to national crises, both natural and man-made.

Organization of This Report

Following Chapter 1, the rest of the report is organized as follows:

- Chapter 2 describes the history of government engagement with HBCUs, TCUs, HSIs, and the communities they serve and provides an overview of common themes from previous National Academies' reports.
- Chapter 3 provides an assessment of the current capabilities of MSIs, the impact of those institutions on STEM education and research, and the current federal funding landscape for MSIs participating in R&D.
- Chapter 4 explores the existing DOD outreach and engagement strategies used across its research programs to engage academic institutions, the current infrastructure for academic research engagement, and programs administered by other federal agencies to support R&D capacity and engagement. It proposes novel opportunities for increasing MSI involvement.
- Chapter 5 outlines assessment strategies for MSI leadership, processes for decision-making and for calculating facilities and administration costs, and potential data collection mechanisms for assessment and identification of MSI capabilities.
- Chapter 6 includes an overview of the committee's recommendations and specifies the roles of MSIs, the defense-related industry, Congress, the DOD, and other federal agencies in the elevation of MSI participation in defense-related R&D.

REFERENCES

Einaudi, P., J. Gordon, and K. Kang. 2022. Baccalaureate origins of underrepresented minority doctorate recipients. InfoBrief, NSF 22-335. National Science Foundation. https://ncses.nsf.gov/pubs/nsf22335/.

Excelencia in Education. 2024. Hispanic-serving institutions (HSIs) factbook: 2022-23. Washington, DC: Excelencia in Education. https://www.edexcelencia.org/media/2502.

Marroquín, C. 2019. Tribal colleges and universities: A testament of resilience and nation-building (CMSI Research Brief). Center for Minority Serving Institutions at the University of Pennsylvania. https://cmsi.gse.rutgers.edu/sites/default/files/TCUs.pdf.

Mazarr, M.J., et al. 2018. *Understanding the emerging era of international competition: Theoretical and historical perspectives.* Santa Monica, CA: RAND Corporation. https://www.rand.org/pubs/research_reports/RR2726.html.

NASEM (National Academies of Sciences, Engineering, and Medicine). 2022. *Defense research capacity at historically black colleges and universities and other minority institutions: Transitioning from good intentions to measurable outcomes.* Washington, DC: The National Academies Press. https://doi.org/10.17226/26399.

NASEM. 2024. *Building defense research capacity at historically black colleges and universities, tribal colleges and universities, and minority-serving institutions: Proceedings of three town halls.* Washington, DC: The National Academies Press. https://doi.org/10.17226/27511.

NCES (National Center for Education Statistics). 2022. Fast facts: Historically black colleges and universities. Institute for Education Sciences, U.S. Department of Education. https://nces.ed.gov/fastfacts/display.asp?id=667.

NRC (National Research Council). 1994. Dual-Use Technologies and Export Control in the Post-Cold War Era. Washington, DC: The National Academies Press. https://doi.org/10.17226/2270. U.S. Census. 2018. Demographic turning points for the United States: Population projections for 2020 to 2060. https://www.census.gov/content/dam/Census/library/publications/2020/demo/p25-1144.pdf.

U.S. Department of Defense. 2022. Department of Defense equity action plan. https://media.defense.gov/2022/Apr/13/2002976515/-1/-1/0/DOD-EQUITY-ACTION-PLAN.PDF.

White House. 2021, September 3. Executive Order on White House Initiative on Advancing Educational Equity, Excellence, and Economic Opportunity through Historically Black Colleges and Universities. https://www.whitehouse.gov/briefing-room/presidential-actions/2021/09/03/executive-order-on-white-house-initiative-on-advancing-educational-equity-excellence-and-economic-opportunity-through-historically-black-colleges-and-universities/.

White House Office of Science & Technology Policy. 2022. Biden-Harris Administration announces historic actions to advance national vision for STEMM equity and excellence. https://www.whitehouse.gov/ostp/news-updates/2022/12/12/biden-harris-administration-announces-historic-actions-to-advance-national-vision-for-stemm-equity-and-excellence/.

Zhang, R. 2024. *Building up research capacity at minority institutions: Report for the National Academy of Sciences.* Commissioned paper for the National Academies' Committee on the Development of a Plan to Promote Defense Research at Historically Black Colleges and Universities, Tribal Colleges and Universities, and Hispanic-Serving Institutions. https://nap.nationalacademies.org/catalog/27838.

Zwetsloot, R., et al. 2021. Data brief: China is fast outpacing U.S. STEM PhD growth. Center for Security and Emerging Technology. https://cset.georgetown.edu/publication/china-is-fast-outpacing-u-s-stem-phd-growth/.

2

Government Engagement with Minority-Serving Institutions: History and Common Themes from Previous Reports

In the early years of the United States, federal and state governments did not play a large role in education. Most Americans left school after Grade 8, if they were fortunate to go that far. An even smaller percentage of the population attended college: about 1 percent of the population in 1869-1870 (the first year for which data are available) and almost exclusively white Protestant men (NCES, 1993). With a few exceptions, the nation's first institutions of higher education (IHEs) were established by religious and private organizations. In 1839, the first public "normal school" to prepare teachers opened in Massachusetts.

The U.S. government first became significantly involved in higher education in 1862 with the passage of what is now called the First Morrill Act.[1] It provided federal funding to states to establish land-grant colleges focused on agricultural and mechanical subjects and included exploring military tactics, all topics of importance to the Department of Defense (DOD). Five years later, in 1867, a federal office of education was established, originally within the Department of the Interior and staffed by a commissioner and three clerks (NCES, 1993). After World War II, as articulated in *Science—the Endless Frontier* (Bush, 1945), the federal government began to invest heavily in science and technology (S&T), both within agencies but especially through support of academic research. While industry funds a higher

---

[1] U.S. Congress. Act of July 2, 1862. First Morrill Act. Enrolled Acts and Resolutions of Congress, 1789-1996. General Records of the United States Government. National Archives.

amount of research than other sectors, it is mostly in the area of experimental development. Through investments in basic and applied research, the federal government funds about 52 percent of research and development (R&D) performed by higher education institutions (NSF, 2024).

Recognizing the large role that the government plays in the higher education landscape, numerous studies by the National Academies of Sciences, Engineering, and Medicine (the National Academies) have looked at government engagement with minority-serving institutions (MSIs). This chapter highlights aspects of that history relevant to the committee's statement of task and summarizes common themes and gaps across previous National Academies' studies.

HISTORY OF GOVERNMENT ENGAGEMENT

Government Designations of MSIs

The first MSIs were the Historically Black Colleges and Universities (HBCUs) that trace their origins prior to the Civil War. Among these are Cheney University and Lincoln University in Pennsylvania, established by private philanthropy respectively in 1837 and 1854. Wilberforce University in Ohio was similarly founded in 1857. The decades following the Civil War saw a flourishing of newly established institutions, both public and private, dedicated to the education of the formerly enslaved and their descendants.

Through the First Morrill Act of 1862, Congress bestowed "land-grant" status to one educational institution per state "to teach such branches of learning as are related to agriculture and the mechanic arts."[2] The new institutions extended higher education to thousands of farmers and other working people, but states could (and did) set their own exclusionary policies as to who could enroll. The Second Morrill Act of 1890 required each state either to admit students without regard to race or to establish a separate land-grand institution for students of color.[3] Rather than admit African American students into their existing institutions, 18 southern states created a second set of land-grant universities, sometimes known as the "1890 Schools." These and other institutions were defined as HBCUs

---

[2] U.S. Congress. Act of July 2, 1862. First Morrill Act. Enrolled Acts and Resolutions of Congress, 1789-1996. General Records of the United States Government. National Archives.

[3] U.S. Congress. Act of August 30, 1890. Second Morrill Act. Enrolled Acts and Resolutions of Congress, 1789-1996. General Records of the United States Government. National Archives.

by the Higher Education Act of 1965: "any historically black college or university that was established prior to 1964, whose principal mission was, and is, the education of black Americans."[4] There are now 107 HBCUs.

Tribal Colleges and Universities (TCUs) were established by individual Native American tribes "to strengthen reservations and tribal culture without assimilation," starting with Navajo Community College (now Diné College) in 1968. TCU-specific federal funding only began through the Tribally Controlled Community College Assistance Act of 1978 (AIHEC, 1999). And although the original Morrill Act was funded through the granting of more than 10 million acres of land expropriated from Native American tribes, Congress did not grant TCUs status as land-grant institutions until 1994, through the Equity in Educational Land-Grant Status Act of 1994. There are now more than 30 TCUs.

In addition to these two historically defined designations, legislation between 1992 and 2008 established criteria for five categories of enrollment-defined or enrollment-driven MSIs:

1. Hispanic-Serving Institutions (HSIs), established through the Higher Education Act of 1992, are institutions with 25 percent or more total undergraduate full-time-equivalent student enrollment of Hispanic students.
2. Asian American and Native American Pacific Islander-Serving Institutions (AANAPISIs), established through the College Cost Reduction and Access Act of 2007, have at least 10 percent enrollment of Asian American or Pacific Islander students.
3. Alaska Native and Native Hawaiian-Serving Institutions, established through the Higher Education Act of 1998, have at least 20 percent Alaska Native students or 10 percent Native Hawaiian students.
4. Predominantly Black Institutions, established through the Higher Education Opportunity Act of 2008, are institutions that are not HBCUs but (1) have at least 1,000 students; (2) have at least 50 percent low-income first-generation-to-college, degree-seeking undergraduate enrollment; (3) have low per-full-time undergraduate expenditure in comparison with other institutions offering similar students; and (4) enroll at least 40 percent African American students.

---

[4] Higher Education Act of 1965, Pub. L. No. 89-329, Title III, Section 322(2), 79 Stat. 1219 (1965).

5. Native American-Serving Nontribal Institutions, also established through the Higher Education Opportunity Act of 2008, are institutions that are not TCUs but have at least 10 percent Native American students.

Because enrollment percentages, expenditures, and other variables can change over time, the U.S. Department of Education's Office of Post-secondary Education maintains a list of these MSIs. Institutions can have more than one designation (e.g., based on enrollment numbers, an institution can be both an HSI and AANAPISI). It is also noteworthy that changes in overall demographics can move an institution into an enrollment-defined designation, with universities in Texas, California, and Arizona, where Latinx populations have increased in recent years, as examples.

Today, there are over 500 HSIs across the United States, ranging from community colleges to comprehensive universities. HSIs represent 60 percent of all MSIs (Collins et al., 2017).

Funding Disparities from the Start

On both the federal and state levels, support to MSIs has lagged support to non-MSIs since the 19th century. For example, early federal legislation to support research (Hatch Act of 1887) and extension (Smith-Lever Act of 1914) at land-grant institutions did not extend to the HBCUs that were established under the Second Morrill Act.[5] It took until 1977 (for research) and 1997 (for extension) to guarantee funding similar to the initial 1862 institutions (Lee and Keys, 2013). Even then, states could apply for waivers to avoid matching federal funds for the 1890 schools, something they were prohibited to do for the 1862 schools. As a result, non-MSI land-grant universities often received greater than the required matching funds from the states, while the 1890s schools fell short. Only recently has the federal government begun holding states accountable for underfunding their public HBCUs (Hunt Institute, 2022) and, in some instances, depriving land-grant HBCUs of their fair allocation of resources designated for the states' land-grant institutions. In FY 2020, 12 of the 19 schools received a full nonfederal match (Congressional Research Service, 2021), but this does not

---

[5] U.S. Congress. Act of August 30, 1890. Second Morrill Act. Enrolled Acts and Resolutions of Congress, 1789-1996. General Records of the United States Government. National Archives.

make up for years of underfunding. In September 2023, the U.S. Secretaries of Agriculture and Education reported a $12 billion disparity in funding between HBCU and non-HBCU land-grant institutions in 16 states in the past 30 years alone (U.S. Department of Education, 2023). It should be noted that the private HBCUs receive little, if any, state funding.

The history of federal funding of TCUs is more inequitable than HBCUs. Through the Tribally Controlled Community College Assistance Act of 1978, the federal government committed to provide TCUs with $8,000 per year per each enrolled Native American student; however, in FY 2015, funds only equaled $6,355 per Native American student (Nelson and Frye, 2016). TCUs are more reliant on federal funding than other public institutions because in most instances, they receive no state tax financial support and are unable or reluctant to levy taxes on their own generally high-poverty populations (Stull et al., 2015). A study of the funding of TCUs using academic year 2013-2014 data showed dramatically different funding between 4-year TCUs and 4-year public, non-TCU institutions (Nelson and Frye, 2016):

- The average TCU received 73.7 percent of its funding from the federal government in the form of direct federal appropriations, grants, and contracts. By contrast, public, 4-year, non-TCUs received just 18.7 percent of their funding from federal sources.
- State appropriations, grants, and contracts were virtually non-existent for TCUs, but provided 33.8 percent of public, non-TCU funding. Only two states (North Dakota and Arizona) allocated funding to TCUs to help support the costs of enrolling both Native and non-Native students.

TCUs receive about 9 percent of their revenues from student tuition and fees, as compared to 37.7 percent for non-TCUs. Moreover, TCU tuition and fees are below the national average, and most provide significant tuition and waivers to meet the financial constraints of their students.

HSIs represent the largest percentage of MSIs, and the number is anticipated to increase in alignment with the national demographic trends reported by the U.S. Census. While HSIs are often celebrated for their commitment to undergraduate education, their research capacity and contributions to the national research ecosystem are less explored and understood. As examined more fully in Chapter 3, National Center for Science and Engineering Statistics data indicate very disparate funding portfolios. A small number (about 3.5 percent of the total) receive 79 percent of federal S&T dollars awarded to High Hispanic Enrollment institutions.

Finding:
- On both the federal and state levels, support to MSIs has lagged behind support to non-MSIs since the 19th century.

THEMES AND GAPS FROM PREVIOUS STUDIES

The committee's statement of task requested that it refer to previous National Academies' reports that assessed the current and potential capabilities of MSIs to participate in defense-related engineering and R&D activities. While not an exhaustive search, the focus was to identify common themes and point to gaps that the current study could address. The committee reviewed reports that studied minority participation in science, technology, engineering, and mathematics (STEM) generally, as well as those focused on the DOD (Box 2-1).

Previous reports have explored themes of challenges and opportunities that persist across MSIs and the communities they serve as efforts are made to increase their STEM footprints. The themes presented here center on the roles that institutions and federal agencies can play toward increased minority engagement in federal R&D. Investigations have highlighted capacity-related challenges within institutions to not only engage in research but also administer grants and make changes related to leadership, the professoriate, and pedagogy. Previous reports have also highlighted the need for federal agencies to provide targeted funding to support MSI infrastructure needs, the development of programs that impact workforce development through support for faculty and students at MSIs, and the creation of mechanisms that support collaborations across MSIs and incentivize increased R&D interactions with larger well-sourced academic institutions such as R1s through more equitable partnerships.

Theme I: Internal Interventions for Better Engagement with Federal R&D

Previous reports identified that a significant factor in how an institution engages with the federal R&D enterprise, defense-related or otherwise, hinges on its ability to develop internal structures that provide an environment for research personnel's success. Strong, forward-looking

---

BOX 2-1
National Academies' Reports on Minority Participation in Science, Technology, Engineering, and Mathematics and Department of Defense Research

- *Examination of the U.S. Air Force's science, technology, engineering, and mathematics workforce needs in the future and its strategy to meet those needs* (2010)
- *Expanding underrepresented minority participation: America's science and technology talent at the crossroads* (2011)
- *Research universities and the future of America: Ten breakthrough actions vital to our nation's prosperity and security* (2012)
- *Assuring the U.S. Department of Defense a strong science, technology, engineering, and mathematics (STEM) workforce* (2012)
- *Seeking solutions: Maximizing American talent by advancing women of color in academia: Summary of a conference* (2013)
- *Barriers and opportunities for 2-year and 4-year STEM degrees: Systemic change to support students' diverse pathways* (2016)
- *Closing the equity gap: Securing our STEM education and workforce readiness in the nation's minority-serving institutions* (2019)
- *Minority serving institutions: America's underutilized resource for strengthening the STEM workforce* (2019)
- *Defense research capacity at historically black colleges and universities and other minority institutions: Transitioning from good intentions to measurable outcomes* (2022)
- *Transforming research and higher education in the next 75 years: Proceedings from the 2022 Endless Frontier Symposium* (2023)

---

leadership with comprehensive strategic planning and the subsequent implementation of those plans can allow institutions to develop nimble systems that can adapt to developing national research priorities and needs. According to several studies, adequate strategic planning should focus on efficient resource allocation to support existing infrastructure. The administration at MSIs interested in expanding DOD research should prioritize investments in internal infrastructure relevant to key areas of STEM across government and industry to ensure that institutional priorities closely align with funding and workforce needs. Moreover, institutions with aspirations to increase their research capabilities should work to modernize processes to increase their productivity through the incorporation of new technologies and management practices and adoption of best practices for operational efficiency. In some instances, outsourcing, centralizing, or sharing research support and resources could increase capacity across multiple MSIs (National Academy of Engineering and National Research Council, 2009, 2012; National Research Council, 2012; NASEM, 2019). Chapter 5 explores a strategic planning methodology that MSIs can explore using an assessment of existing assets.

Academic institutions seeking to develop a more effective and engaged R&D ecosystem must tackle faculty recruitment, retention, and development to sustain their strategic efforts, these studies recommend. Necessary faculty support mechanisms for MSIs are wide-ranging, requiring interventions that address the institution's mission and the needs of the faculty. To recruit research-capable faculty, institutions must develop competitive compensation and startup funds commensurate with the compensation provided at larger institutions within their vicinity. MSIs must also administer policies that address barriers to engaging in research, such as prohibitive teaching loads that require faculty at MSIs to teach three to five classes per semester. Finally, enhancing faculty development through the introduction of development programs and research-engaged sabbaticals will support skill development and help foster leadership in research. Formalized mentoring will ensure that the environment at a given institution supports the success of industrious research-capable faculty populations (National Academy of Engineering and National Research Council, 2009; NASEM, 2019, 2022).

Developing a strong culture of administrative leadership and research-engaged faculty will support the development of the next generation, ensuring that students at MSIs can successfully pursue careers and advanced degrees in STEM relevant to federal R&D priorities. Many MSIs are 2-year degree-granting institutions; introducing and broadening existing articulation pathways among MSIs and across IHEs will assist in the lifetime success of their student populations. These pathways must provide training and exposure to opportunities for engagement in federal R&D and embed preparation for obtaining security clearances to support and conduct classified research. With appropriate support, institutions can enhance existing curricula with intentional reforms that support a diverse student population by providing research experiences, mentoring, and other evidence-based STEM engagement structures. Furthermore, institutions must develop and coordinate co-curricula that leverage technology and external expertise in key STEM areas (National Academy of Sciences, National Academy of Engineering, and Institute of Medicine, 2011; National Research Council, 2013; NASEM, 2016).

A major challenge identified in several studies is that while MSIs have committed leaders, dedicated faculty, enthusiastic students, and proud alumni, they lack the capital resources that are critical to establish, support, and scale up the most effective programs (e.g., NASEM, 2019). A common point of pride among MSI leaders is that investments made in these institutions result in a higher return on investment than a similar investment made at a non-MSI. But as with the wrestler or boxer constantly fighting above their weight class, it is an exhausting battle, as related in previous reports. For each success story, long days are needed to put out both figurative and even literal fires due to delayed maintenance resulting from years of underfunding.

Findings from Previous Reports:
- MSIs seeking to develop a more effective and engaged R&D ecosystem must tackle faculty recruitment, retention, and development to sustain their strategic efforts.
- Many MSIs are 2-year degree-granting institutions; introducing and broadening existing articulation pathways within MSIs and across all IHEs will assist in the lifetime success of their student populations.

Theme II: External Investments and Strategies to Support MSI Research

Federal, state, and local governments have a long history of supporting the research infrastructure at IHEs. Unfortunately, MSIs have disproportionately gone under-resourced and underutilized in the national R&D landscape. Previous reports have highlighted that underinvestment at the state and federal levels prevents the full breadth of the U.S. R&D ecosystem from active, meaningful participation. To address this underinvestment, both federal and state governments must provide equitable and adequate funding coupled with autonomy for research-engaged or aspiring institutions. Further government funding and policies should be provided in a stable fashion that fosters innovation and growth toward better engagement in national R&D priorities.

Previous studies have also specified the need for federal agencies to administer targeted investments. These investments should center on existing barriers and challenges and provide opportunities for growth. Investments can provide funding for physical infrastructure and major instrumentation, support growth in MSI administrative infrastructure, and introduce funding for faculty development and financial support for students pursuing degrees in STEM priority fields. Furthermore, federal agencies that provide research grant funding and support STEM education programs should improve their data collection and analysis activities to integrate efficiency and better evaluation of the outcomes of federal research intervention investments toward more effective programs. To ensure the sustainability and effectiveness of efforts, an interagency task force facilitated by the White House or central organizing body should be developed to oversee and improve agency policies and regulatory frameworks for the increased participation of MSIs in federal R&D.

More needs to be done to undergird strong government, university, and industry partnerships to sustain investments and growth in research, previous National Academies' studies have urged. Workforce development and R&D need more effective collaborative frameworks between academic institutions, industry, and government to better integrate with national priorities. These frameworks should incentivize joint research initiatives that leverage the faculty and students of MSIs and facilitate investments in an institution's infrastructure and needs. These partnerships will provide the students with practical experiences in industry and federal labs to ensure the proper development of participants in the relevant STEM ecosystems. This multisectoral environment will ensure that there is not only an increase in diversity of STEM workers but also a feedback loop of capacity development at MSIs.

Workforce development is in the DNA of MSIs. This often leads the DOD and other entities to see the main value proposition of MSIs to be talent pipelines (NASEM, 2022). While this is an important contribution, making investments in the pipeline, and not just tapping into it to select individual students, is critical to forming true partnerships. STEM degrees can be more expensive and take longer to obtain than non-STEM degrees. Creative programs such as the Defense Civilian Training Corps already exist to provide valuable scholarships while opening the pipeline beyond those who want to wear the uniform and join Reserve Officers' Training Corps programs (U.S. Department of Defense, 2024). The DOD also has its own job training sites such as the War College and Navy Post Graduate School. These types of programs could be linked to undergraduate programs at institutions to add advanced skills and training as well as appeal to students considering a DOD pathway.

Finally, as the reports point out, the country needs "all hands on deck" to meet the nation's future STEM needs. Women in STEM and specifically women of color in STEM require intentional and targeted attention (National Research Council, 2013). Women of color are more likely to work at MSIs, providing a mentoring pipeline for female students. A female student is more likely to choose a career pathway if she has contact with a female professor in that pathway. Involving women in the DOD research and training enterprise will open access to an underrepresented perspective of ideas that will help secure the future of the DOD.

Finding from Previous Reports:
To ensure the sustainability and effectiveness of efforts, an interagency task force should be developed to oversee and improve agency policies and regulatory frameworks for the increased participation of MSIs in federal R&D.

RECOMMENDATION 2-1: The systemic underinvestment in R&D capacity at MSIs, particularly in their infrastructure at the state and federal levels, is a pressing issue. To capture the full potential of MSIs, it is imperative that the DOD, with congressional support, introduce mechanisms for dedicated funding for non-R1 MSIs to foster research infrastructure growth including funding facilities and equipment. Potential forms of support could include the following:

- Providing direct support for investment in facilities and equipment to increase R&D relevant to national needs for MSIs such as TCUs, which span multiple states, and private HBCUs, which receive less state support than their public counterparts.
- Providing matching funds for states to invest in research infrastructure growth at MSIs seeking to increase their research infrastructure. These matching funds will incentivize state and local governments that have fallen short of authorizations, which has led to systemic and inequitable underinvestment in MSIs.

REFERENCES

Bush, V. 1945. *Science—the endless frontier: A report to the President by Vannevar Bush, Director of the Office of Scientific Research and Development*, July 1945. United States Government Printing Office, Washington.

Collins, T.W., S.E. Grineski, J. Shenberger, X. Morales, O.F. Morera, and L.E. Echegoyen. 2017. Undergraduate research participation is associated with improved student outcomes at a Hispanic-serving institution. *Journal of College Student Development, 58*(4), 583-600.

Congressional Research Service. 2021. 1890 Land-grant universities: Background and selected issues. https://crsreports.congress.gov/product/pdf/IF/IF11847/2.

Hunt Institute. 2022. Addressing historic underfunding of HBCUs: Implementing bipartisan legislation in Tennessee. https://hunt-institute.org/wp-content/uploads/2022/12/2022.12.6_THI_HE_LuminaBrief3.pdf.

Lee, J.M., and S.W. Keys. 2013. Land-grant but unequal: State one-to-one match funding for 1890 land-grant universities. https://www.aplu.org/wp-content/uploads/land-grant-but-unequal-state-one-to-one-match-funding-for-1890-land-grant-universities.pdf.

NASEM (National Academies of Sciences, Engineering, and Medicine). 2016. *Barriers and opportunities for 2-year and 4-year STEM degrees: Systemic change to support students' diverse pathways.* Washington, DC: The National Academies Press. https://doi.org/10.17226/21739.

NASEM. 2019. *Minority serving institutions: America's underutilized resource for strengthening the STEM workforce.* Washington, DC: The National Academies Press. https://doi.org/10.17226/25257.

NASEM. 2022. *Defense research capacity at historically black colleges and universities and other minority institutions: Transitioning from good intentions to measurable outcomes.* Washington, DC: The National Academies Press. https://doi.org/10.17226/26399.

NASEM. 2023. *Transforming research and higher education institutions in the next 75 years: Proceedings of the 2022 Endless Frontier Symposium.* Washington, DC: The National Academies Press. https://doi.org/10.17226/26863.

National Academy of Engineering and National Research Council. 2009. *Partnerships for emerging research institutions: Report of a workshop.* Washington, DC: The National Academies Press. https://doi.org/10.17226/12577.

National Academy of Engineering and National Research Council. 2012. *Assuring the U.S. Department of Defense a strong science, technology, engineering, and mathematics (STEM) workforce.* Washington, DC: The National Academies Press. https://doi.org/10.17226/13467.

National Academy of Sciences, National Academy of Engineering, and Institute of Medicine. 2011. *Expanding underrepresented minority participation: America's science and technology talent at the crossroads.* Washington, DC: The National Academies Press. https://doi.org/10.17226/12984.

National Research Council. 2010. *Examination of the U.S. Air Force's science, technology, engineering, and mathematics (STEM) workforce needs in the future and its strategy to meet those needs.* Washington, DC: The National Academies Press. https://doi.org/10.17226/12718.

National Research Council. 2012. *Research universities and the future of America: Ten break-through actions vital to our nation's prosperity and security.* Washington, DC: The National Academies Press. https://doi.org/10.17226/13396.

National Research Council. 2013. *Seeking solutions: Maximizing American talent by advancing women of color in academia: Summary of a conference.* Washington, DC: The National Academies Press. https://doi.org/10.17226/18556.

NCES (National Center for Education Statistics). 1993. 120 years of American education: A statistical portrait. Institute for Education Sciences, U.S. Department of Education. https://nces.ed.gov/pubs93/93442.pdf.

Nelson, C.A., and J.R. Frye. 2016. Tribal college and university funding: Tribal sovereignty at the intersection of federal, state, and local funding. American Council on Education & Center for Policy Research and Strategy. https://www.acenet.edu/Documents/Tribal-College-and-University-Funding.pdf.

NSF (National Science Foundation). 2024. The state of U.S. science and engineering, 2024. National Center for Science and Engineering Statistics. https://ncses.nsf.gov/indicators.

Stull, G., et al. 2015. Redefining success: How tribal colleges and universities build nations, strengthen sovereignty, and persevere through challenges. Penn Center for Minority Serving Institutions. https://repository.upenn.edu/server/api/core/bitstreams/2a615606-674f-4991-989d-17ab866d65e9/content.

U.S. Department of Defense. 2024. Defense Civilian Training Corps. OUSD Acquisition & Sustainment. https://dctc.mil/.

U.S. Department of Education. 2023. Secretaries of Education, Agriculture call on governors to equitably fund land-grant HBCUs. https://www.ed.gov/news/press-releases/secretaries-education-agriculture-call-governors-equitably-fund-land-grant-hbcus.

3

Outlining Opportunities at MSIs: An Assessment of the Capabilities of Minority-Serving Institutions

Minority-serving institutions (MSIs), including Historically Black Colleges and Universities (HBCUs), Tribal Colleges and Universities (TCUs), and Hispanic-Serving Institutions (HSIs), offer a range of expertise and perspectives to the Department of Defense (DOD) and other agencies involved in defense-related research. Many currently are, or could be, positioned to fill key gaps in DOD research and to contribute to a diverse domestic science, technology, engineering, and mathematics (STEM) workforce. This chapter examines the capabilities of MSIs through the lens of the Carnegie Classification of Institutions of Higher Education system; a mapping of MSIs' Classification of Instructional Programs (CIP) against the DOD's Critical Technology Areas (CTAs); and information from open information-gathering sessions, a commissioned paper, site visits to three institutions, and responses to a Request for Information (RFI).

MSI CAPABILITIES AND CHARACTERISTICS

More than two decades ago, the Educational Testing Service (ETS) issued a report that pointed to the underrepresentation of Black and Hispanic STEM students in higher education. Presciently, the report (Barton, 2002) looked at the nation's demographic trends and national security needs to pose, "What does all of this portend for the adequacy of the pool of talent from which we can draw our scientists and engineers, and for increasing the representation of minorities in these professions?" The ensuing years have borne out the relevancy of this question. By 2040, the United States will be majority-minority: that is, a majority of Americans will not be white. This is already true for Americans under the age of 18 (U.S. Census Bureau, 2023*).* Although the ETS report was published in the early 2000s, it could have been addressed to the national security establishment today, which remains concerned with recruitment for the all-volunteer military and for talent qualified for classified national security work. Enhancing capacity at pertinent colleges and universities directly addresses the talent concerns for protection of the nation.

Approximately 800 MSIs across the country educate talent in fields pertaining to STEM, social sciences, and humanities in service to the domestic and international agenda of the United States. These fields include the modern languages, the social and behavioral sciences, the natural sciences, and engineering. All are essential to the mission of the DOD and other national security agencies. As detailed in previous National Academies' reports, MSIs represent an underutilized and underappreciated asset in growing the STEM workforce (NASEM, 2019; see also Chapters 1 and 2). These institutions are essential to meeting the nation's need for talent in STEM and other essential disciplines.

Some MSIs often serve underserved demographics such as non-traditional students, older students, veterans, and individuals who identify as disabled. For example, the average age of students at Tohono O'odham Community College was 33 years old in 2023 (Tohono O'odham Community College, 2023). At Iḷisaġvik College in Northern Alaska, 63 percent of students were older than 25 in 2023 (Iḷisaġvik College, 2023).

There is substantial diversity among MSIs related to mission, size, resources, location, STEM programs, and other characteristics. TCUs, for example, are generally very small institutions. Many have student enrollment in the low hundreds and staff in the dozens. Also, many TCUs are geographically remote, often more than 100 miles from an urban center. Sinte Gleska University on the Rosebud Indian Reservation, for example, is 168 miles from Rapid City and 224 miles from Sioux Falls, South Dakota. In a 2021 report, the Minority Business Development Agency characterizes these locations as "education deserts."

The HBCUs include community colleges and baccalaureate institutions primarily focused on teaching and others with significant research activity. Research at these institutions is funded by a range of federal agencies. Primarily undergraduate institutions, such as Spelman College and Xavier University of Louisiana, support significant research activity embedded within their instructional missions. Others, such as Clark Atlanta University and North Carolina Agricultural and Technical State University, also grant Ph.D.s in STEM and other disciplines. All these contribute to new knowledge and prepare needed talent.

Some state university MSIs embrace their roles serving minority students. For example, the University of Alaska has a formal Alaska Native success initiative that includes a goal to "recruit and hire Indigenous faculty and staff to have a workforce that reflects our Alaska Native population which is about 20 percent in the state" (University of Alaska System, 2024). Through existing STEM programs (including the Alaska Native Science and Engineering Program at the University of Alaska, Anchorage), paired with support programs specifically aimed at Alaska Native students, the university has documented STEM success, including an eightfold increase in the annual number of bachelor's degrees in engineering awarded to Alaska Native or American Indian students from 2000 to 2016 (University of Alaska Anchorage, 2019). The university has documented that Alaska Native/American Indian students in these programs have an 8.2 percent higher retention rate and a 4.6 percent higher 5-year graduation rate than those Alaska Native/American Indian students not participating in supportive programs.

HSIs, as noted earlier, represent a growing, diverse proportion of the MSI landscape. Several are large institutions that have gained an MSI designation as Latinx populations in their region or state have increased. Significant disparities in research and development (R&D) funding, however, persist among HSIs.

According to Higher Education Research and Development (HERD) Survey data, the R&D expenditure rates of HSIs represent about 10 percent of all R&D expenditures annually (Table 3-1), but there is a large difference between the number of HSIs that are R1s and those that are not R1s.

Table 3-2 demonstrates the distribution of federal obligations for science and engineering (S&E) funding. Seventy-nine percent of all federally obligated S&E funding to High Hispanic Enrollment colleges and universities was awarded to 18 R1 institutions out of 185 listed HSIs. Only $735 million was awarded to the other 167 HSIs engaged in S&E research in FY2021.

TABLE 3-1 HSIs' R&D Expenditures

	2022	2021	2020	2019	2018
All R&D (million $)	97,842	89,833	86,440	83,643	79,174
All HSI R&D	10,047 (10%)	9,322 (10%)	8,966 (10%)	8,356 (10%)	7,868 (9.94%)
Non-R1 HSI R&D	834 (.85%)	742 (.83%)	748 (.87%)	760 (.91%)	706 (.89%)

SOURCE: Committee-generated, based on National Center for Science and Engineering Statistics data.

TABLE 3-2 Federal Obligations for S&E Funding by Institution (FY2021)

U. Illinois, Chicago	299,000
U. Texas, Austin	270,453
U. Arizona	261,376
U. California, Irvine	258,585
U. Texas M. D. Anderson Cancer Center	210,727
U. California, Santa Barbara	185,654
Arizona State U.	184,688
U. Texas Health Science Center, Houston	161,199
U. Texas Health Science Center, San Antonio	138,088
U. New Mexico	133,471
U. Central Florida	121,234
U. California, Riverside	108,245
U. Texas Medical Branch at Galveston	102,749
Texas A&M U., College Station	90,553
U. California, Santa Cruz	75,189
Florida International U.	67,851
Northern Arizona U.	57,505
U. Houston	46,448
All other HSIs (n=167)	735

SOURCE: Committee-generated, based on National Center for Science and Engineering Statistics data.

CARNEGIE CLASSIFICATIONS AND
THE EVOLVING DEFINITION OF "RESEARCH ACTIVE"

In 1973, the Carnegie Commission on Higher Education proposed a classification system to categorize degree-granting institutions in the United States (Carnegie Classification of Institutions of Higher Education, 2024). Updated periodically since then, the Carnegie Classification of Institutions of Higher Education, according to its website, "is used in the study of higher education and [is] intended to be an objective, degree-based lens through which researchers can group and study similar institution." Based on data from the Integrated Postsecondary Education Data System (IPEDS), inputs include numbers of undergraduates, extent of graduate program, and size of research portfolio. The six Carnegie Classifications range from "special focus institutions" (such as a music conservatory or religious institution) to "doctoral universities." Doctoral universities can be classified with "very high research activity," known as R1; "high research activity," known as R2; and "doctoral/professional," known as R3. According to the most recent classification (2021), 11 HSIs and no HBCUs were R1s; 12 HSIs and 11 HBCUs were R2s; and 15 HSIs and 16 HBCUs were R3s. Many of the HSIs with an R1 classification are large public universities with robust research funding in states with high Latinx populations (e.g., institutions in the Texas and California university systems). TCUs are not included in the Carnegie Classification system.

As the committee heard during open sessions, the next iteration of the Carnegie Classification, scheduled for release in early 2025, will have major changes in how the classification thresholds are determined (ACE, 2023). In addition, the Carnegie Classifications will incorporate the impact of institutions of higher education (IHEs) on social and economic mobility as part of assessing an institution's impact and capabilities. One expectation is that at least one HBCU will be designated an R1, along with several additional HSIs, and a number of HBCUs and HSIs will be designated as R2s.

Although not an explicit intention of the system, an institution classified as an R1 receives significant prestige within and outside the academic ecosystem, being described as a top tier research university that can conduct the most cutting-edge research and provide high-quality instruction. Many universities dedicate considerable resources to reaching or maintaining R1 or R2 status. Part of the committee's task was to address how MSIs can achieve R1 status. Many of the recommendations contained in this report can contribute to this goal for institutions that are on that pathway.

As a system for describing large, well-funded academic institutions, the Carnegie Classifications are well-situated to provide a cursory assessment of the research capabilities of R1 and R2 institutions. However, the Carnegie Classifications have fallen short in providing an assessment of the unique contributions that institutions that fall below the R1/R2 thresholds can provide the U.S. R&D ecosystem. R1s account for approximately 4 percent of all U.S. IHEs, which means that the vast majority of U.S. students pursuing undergraduate and postgraduate education do so at a non-R1 institution. Non-R1 institutions include a diversity of schools that serve rural communities, returning learners, Indigenous and African American communities, and other populations that have much to offer the DOD. Robust R&D engagement occurs at non-R1s. Thus, while R1 and R2 designation is important for many institutions, targeting resources to a broader array of MSIs will expand capacity and provide an opportunity to increase the diversity of perspectives engaging throughout the U.S. R&D landscape.

Findings:

- According to the most recent Carnegie Classification of Institutions of Higher Education (2021), 11 HSIs and no HBCUs were R1s; 12 HSIs and 11 HBCUs were R2s; and 15 HSIs and 16 HBCUs were R3s. TCUs are not included in the Carnegie Classification system, and many of the HSIs with an R1 classification are large public universities with robust research funding in states with high Latinx populations (e.g., institutions in the Texas and California university systems).
- Given reforms in the Carnegie Classification system, it is expected that at least one HBCU will be designated as an R1 institution, along with several additional HSIs, and a number of HBCUs and HSIs will be designated as R2s in 2025.

NATIONAL SECURITY NEEDS, DOD PRIORITIES, AND MSI CAPABILITIES

The DOD's Office of the Under Secretary of Defense for Research and Engineering has outlined 14 CTAs that will ensure that the nation maintains its competitive advantage globally and is prepared to address future research, development, and security needs. Institutions may find significant opportunities to engage in the full breadth of the Department's R&D

ecosystem across basic and applied research infrastructure by mapping their existing S&E programs to these CTAs:

- Biotechnology
- Quantum Science
- Future Generation Wireless Technology
- Advanced Materials
- Trusted AI and Autonomy
- Integrated Network Systems-of-Systems
- Microelectronics
- Space Technology
- Renewable Energy Generation and Storage
- Advanced Computing and Software
- Human-Machine Interfaces
- Direct Energy
- Hypersonics
- Integrated Sensing and Cyber

To assess the current capabilities of MSIs to educate and engage in the DOD's CTAs, the study committee reviewed the National Center for Education Statistics (NCES) CIP codes.[1] CIP codes provide insight into existing programs at IHEs and can allow organizations to identify institutions that are currently providing degrees in these fields. Looking across the CIPs, the committee agreed that five general fields of study in the CIP relate closely to the DOD's CTAs.[2] According to the committee's analysis of NCES data, 89 percent of HBCUs have at least one program relevant to the DOD's needs, and 62.5 percent of TCUs have existing programs relevant to the CTAs. Mapping CIP codes with CTAs, however, requires additional inputs to fully assess the current and existing capabilities of MSIs, such as setting thresholds for the number of programs that exist at MSIs currently and identifying the level of resources applied to relevant DOD programs

---

[1] See Classification of Instructional Programs Codes, https://nces.ed.gov/ipeds/cipcode/resources.aspx?y=56.

[2] The specific CIP codes analyzed were Engineering (60); Engineering/Engineering-related Technologies/Technicians (77); Physical Sciences (45); Biological and Physical Sciences, Physical Sciences, General, Social Sciences (40); Social Sciences, General, Computer Science, Linguistics and Computer Science, Mathematics and Computer Science, Biochemical Engineering, Chemical Engineering, Chemical Engineering Technology/Technician, Chemical Engineering, Other.

to highlight opportunities for increased support that can facilitate access to skill development for students across MSIs.

Findings:
- More than 800 MSIs across the country educate talent in STEM, social sciences, and humanities and may serve the U.S. domestic and international agenda for defense and national security.
- Targeting resources to a broader array of MSIs will expand capacity and provide an opportunity to increase the diversity of perspectives being engaged throughout the U.S. R&D landscape.
- According to the committee's analysis, 89 percent of HBCUs have at least one program relevant to the DOD's needs, and 62.5 percent of TCUs have existing programs relevant to the DOD's CTAs.

ADDITIONAL INPUTS ON MSI CAPABILITIES AND OPPORTUNITIES

The committee commissioned a paper from an independent researcher (Zhang, 2024) to characterize the current research capacity of MSIs and explore potential avenues of investment. To review institutional R&D activity, the author drew from two datasets from the National Science Foundation (NSF): the HERD Survey and the Survey of Science and Engineering Research Facilities. The HERD Survey, conducted annually, collects information on R&D expenditures at U.S. colleges and universities broken down by field and expenditure type. The S&E Research Facilities survey, conducted biennially, collects information on the amount of space and costs for R&D facilities, also broken down by field. The HERD and Facilities surveys collect data on all U.S. academic institutions reporting at least $150,000 (National Science Foundation, 2022a) and $1 million (National Science Foundation, 2022b) in R&D expenditures in the previous fiscal year, respectively. Thus, not all MSIs are included in these NSF data.

The commissioned paper also analyzed the data through a geographic lens. Previous National Academies' reports have recommended the development of meaningful partnerships between MSIs and other institutions, particularly R1s (stressing that these should be mutually beneficial and not check-the-box arrangements by the larger institutions by providing an equal exchange in research attribution, funding, personnel, and resources). While the data and analysis required to match institutions were beyond the scope of the report, the paper presented preliminary findings from available

IPEDS data to show that most MSIs are not close to an R1 or R2 university. Disregarding own-institution status, HBCUs have a median distance of 30 miles to an R1 and 50 miles to an R2 (see Table 3-3). The median distance between a TCU and an R1 is 174 miles. Around 30 percent of HBCUs have an R1 within 5 miles, while only 12 percent of HSIs have an R1 within 5 miles. There is only one TCU with an R1 located within 5 miles.

There are no outcomes data to empirically verify if co-location with an R1 or R2 augments research output for MSIs. While fruitful partnerships can develop across the miles (e.g., the Princeton-HBCU alliance presented at one of the Town Halls), a reasonable assumption is that proximity facilitates collaboration. Future studies could incorporate collaborative research outputs or faculty/student mobility data to directly measure the impacts of geographical proximity between MSIs and R1/R2 institutions on research capacity. Another aspect to examine is proximity of MSIs to federally funded R&D centers, military installations, and other facilities (see also Chapter 4). As an example, at a Town Hall, a presenter described how Fayetteville State University, although located in a rural area, takes advantage of its location near Fort Liberty (formerly Fort Bragg), one of the largest military bases in the nation.

The paper also looked at three general areas of research capacity delineated by the amount of investments required (e.g., labs, instrumentation, high-performance computing) to make the following observations related to MSI research potential:

TABLE 3-3 Summary Statistics of MSI Distance to R1 and R2 Universities

Measures	HBCU	HSI	TCU
Median Miles to Closest R1	30	42	174
	(115)	(362)	(319)
Institutions with an R1 within 5 Miles	28	40	1
Institutions with an R1 within 10 Miles	39	81	1
Median Miles to Closest R2	50	57	187
	(116)	(364)	(117)
Institutions with an R2 within 5 Miles	14	38	1
Institutions with an R2 within 10 Miles	18	71	1
Total	100	331	35

SOURCE: Zhang, 2024.

- *Investment-Heavy Fields*: Life sciences require intense investment in R&D funding, equipment, and facility space. Engineering and physical sciences also require significant investment in these areas. These investment requirements have proven and will continue to prove difficult for many MSIs to compete with R1s. A possible avenue for growth is strategic partnerships between MSIs and R1s for fields that require large capital investments.
- *Investment-Light Fields*: Math and statistics, psychology, and social sciences require much less investment in R&D funding, equipment, and facility space. This may be an area for MSIs to grow their research capacity.
- *Fields on the Rise*: Computer science is on the rise for R1 spending, especially in equipment and facility space. This is not surprising given the increasing importance of computer science in the past two decades on topics such as cybersecurity and the protection of data. Geosciences and agricultural sciences also show much less differential between R1 and MSI spending.

Institutional objectives are a critical driver for funding decisions. The top 10 HBCUs in terms of R&D spending and facility space tend to be more specialized than the top 10 HSIs in these areas, which may call for different strategies of increasing research investment. Among HSIs, there are more than 300 institutions with a much more heterogeneous distribution than the 11 HSI R1s. MSIs also have a community-driven mission, and it is thus important to determine to what extent expanding research capacity across all fields versus specializing in a few fields is the goal. Additionally, assessing the role to which novel strategies, such as investing in local industries and community partners, can support increased engagement of MSIs may provide unique opportunities for the DOD and institutions with more community-driven missions.

Findings:
- HBCUs have a median distance of 30 miles to an R1 and 50 miles to an R2. The median distance between a TCU and an R1 is 174 miles. Around 30 percent of HBCUs have an R1 within 5 miles, while only 12 percent of HSIs have an R1 within 5 miles. There is only one TCU with an R1 located within 5 miles. While there are no current studies on the relationship of research capacity to proximity, investigating the potential relationships between

neighboring institutions may identify strategies to increase the engagement of MSIs in R&D.

- The top 10 HBCUs in terms of R&D spending and facility space tend to be more specialized than the top 10 HSIs in these areas, which may call for different strategies to increase research investment. Among HSIs, there are more than 300 institutions with a much more heterogeneous distribution than the 11 HSIs that have R1 status.

Town Halls and Site Visits

Two series of public sessions informed the committee, as noted in Chapter 1. In late 2023, the committee held three open sessions to learn about the DOD, other federal, and nonprofit models of engagement with MSIs that might be applied elsewhere (see Appendix A for the agendas and Chapter 4 for highlights).

As a related but discrete effort to this consensus study, the DOD previously supported a series of Town Halls (highlighted below and in NASEM, 2024). Their goal was to further explore key questions that emerged from the 2022 report and to build on its recommendations related to "building research capacity" and developing "true partnerships" between MSIs, other IHEs, and federal agencies. They were held in Washington, DC; Albuquerque, NM; and Chicago, IL. The committee examined the proceedings of those Town Halls.

In addition, subsets of the committee made site visits to Fayetteville State University, Diné College, and California State University at Bakersfield.

Themes that resonated across the committee briefings, Town Halls, and site visits included the following:

- **The need for a long-term view**: Capacity building and partnership development take time and need sustained resources and patience. Several presenters stressed that research infrastructure should be built over time, with adequate resources for maintenance and training. Similarly, partnerships are created and nurtured over time. A number of MSI representatives shared their frustration when R1s and other larger organizations contact them for a quick sign-off for a partnership that exists in name only.

- **Value of consortia**: Consortia facilitate access to education, publications, conferences, and networking, which particularly helps early career researchers. Examples included the South Big Data Innovation Hub, Applied Research Initiative for Mathematics and Computational Sciences, and the HBCU Science and Technology Council. Nonprofits and philanthropic organizations can serve as convenors of these consortia.

- **Considerations of smaller institutions**: Presenters from smaller institutions shared their frustration when agencies are reluctant to provide infrastructure support because it will serve a smaller number of students and faculty. Equipment is essential in running many programs, and excluding these institutions also marginalizes potential STEM talent. Several presenters from smaller institutions appreciated the mentorship provided by larger, more well-resourced schools, but they also stressed the value of peer-to-peer information exchange. In addition, several described situations in which their students and faculty were involved in partnerships with larger institutions, only to have them recruited away to these larger places.

- **Institutional constraints**: Heavy teaching loads were often cited as an obstacle to growing research capacity. Faculty need time to connect with the DOD and other partners, attend conferences, and be proactive in scouting research opportunities, something that is difficult to do while teaching as many as four or five courses a semester. Several presenters noted that their institutions do not have a Ph.D. cohort—the California system that distinguishes between research and teaching-focused institutions was brought up by several presenters. Suggested work-arounds included using postdocs, lab managers, undergraduates, and community college students and leveraging novel opportunities to engage with funders such as participating in virtual meetings with program staff.

- **Administrative capacity**: A common obstacle is the lack of research infrastructure, including staff who are trained to manage federal grants and contracts and capitalize on commercialization and intellectual opportunities. Several participants from state-funded institutions saw funding decrease in recent years. Less-resourced institutions do not have the same level of support as better-resourced institutions, putting them at a further disadvantage.

- **Regional focus**: Several presenters explained that their students are primarily from the local regions and want to remain there for their careers. The DOD and other defense-related facilities in these areas can take advantage of this preference by forging meaningful relationships with students early in their academic pathways.

RECOMMENDATION 3-1: For MSIs to contribute more fully to defense-related research, research capacity and talent must be developed and strengthened. This is a unique strategic opportunity for the DOD and national security. Many MSIs (in particular TCUs) embody distinctive perspectives and so have the potential to make completely unique research contributions in areas such as addressing agricultural systems that are resilient in drought conditions. These distinctive ways of thinking, problem-solving, and social organization should be of interest to both the DOD and the broader scientific community. Investing in investigators at non-R1 MSIs will not only increase the defense-related research capacity base nationally, but also deepen and diversify the available investigators that can support and advance the Department's R&D needs.

- **To partially engage this opportunity, the DOD, with support from Congress, should develop and administer a DOD MSI Investigator Award for very capable scholars at HBCUs, TCUs, and MSIs. This new program should be modeled after existing department programs such as the DARPA Young Faculty Award, Air Force Young Investigator Program, and ONR Young Investigator Program. In the implementation of DOD MSI Investigator awards, the following factors should be included:**
- **Up to 100 awards made per year across the Department's branches (Air Force, Navy, Army, etc.).**
- **Tracking of the number of awards made to each institution type to guide evaluation, outreach, and programmatic planning.**
- **An average of $150,000 per grant per year over a 5-year grant period with the option to renew. This sustained funding will include funding that enables each DOD MSI Investigator**

to establish a research lab at their institution, pursue topics relevant to the DOD's R&D needs, and serve as a focal point for increased engagement for defense-related research.

- Cohorts of investigators should be convened in-person on an annual basis to discuss successes, roadblocks, and recommendations to refine and reshape this program based on the unique and not-well-understood challenges and opportunities at their sites with the identification appropriate metrics for evaluation.
- The focus should be on faculty at HBCUs, TCUs, and non-R1 MSIs with award recipients providing 51 percent of their effort to the funded research project during the duration of the award. The National Institutes of Health PIONEER award and Howard Hughes Medical Institute Program may serve as models for an agency-wide program that supports promising scientists across career stages in addressing high-risk/high-reward issues relevant to the DOD's mission.
- The DOD should avoid the use of 'tenure track" designated faculty as a criterion. The use of "tenure track" appointments creates a barrier for engagement for smaller institutions such as TCUs. As a result, any program focused on developing researchers at non-R1 MSIs that use "tenure track" as an eligibility criterion would preclude both their engagement from these institutions and the DOD from broadening its potential researcher base.
- Review criteria and processes should be developed with an advisory council that includes researchers and research administrators from MSIs and institutions with historical engagement with the DOD.

RECOMMENDATION 3-2: To support the existing missions of MSIs to educate and provide support for investigator release time, the DOD should develop a postdoctoral fellowship program for MSIs geared toward doctoral recipients with specialized expertise in defense-related research areas, broad disciplinary understanding, and interest in developing instructional skills. Funding that provides relief for course and research support at MSIs will help incentivize institutions where teaching loads prohibit significant engagement in research. It can also help support the careers of postdocs pursuing experience as faculty. The DOD should incorporate the following into the program:

- Recipients can allot 50 percent of their time as a research associate within the lab of a faculty member conducting defense-related research and 50 percent of their time to teach courses typically covered by the investigator.
- The duration of the fellowship should correspond with the length of a typical research grant to ensure continuity in course coverage. It should be affixed to non-R1 primary teaching institutions and DOD-relevant MSI funding mechanisms.
- A matching mechanism that connects prospective fellows with MSI faculty should facilitate awarded fellows' identification of a supervising investigator.
- A postdoctoral mentoring plan should be included. Mentoring plans should be standardized to ensure continuity in support for fellows, and mentors should receive training on mentorship.

Responses from the RFI

As part of this study, the committee issued an RFI to better understand institutions' research ecosystems. The survey received more than 50 responses. While not a statistically rigorous sample, the responses provide an illuminating snapshot of how institutions see themselves, and administering similar information requests periodically may assist in providing a more comprehensive view of MSI research ecosystems. Respondents encompassed broad coverage of Carnegie Classifications as well as significant diversity related to location and size of the student body, from several hundred to more than 50,000 students. Each has a significant percentage of faculty involved in at least one, and usually all or most, of the six CIP areas mentioned above.

While all respondents indicated they have research within their strategic plan, the extent to which the institution conducted research with DOD support varied greatly. A variety of different roles currently engage with the DOD, including vice presidents of research through sponsored program offices, administrators, department chairs, principal investigators, and others (Figure 3-1).[3]

---

[3] The committee referred to the definition "principal investigator" in 2 CFR § 1108.295 – "The single individual whom an organization that is carrying out a research project with DOD support designates as having an appropriate level of authority and responsibility for leading and directing the research intellectually and logistically, which includes the proper conduct of the research, the appropriate use of funds, and compliance with administrative requirements such as the submission of performance reports to the DOD."

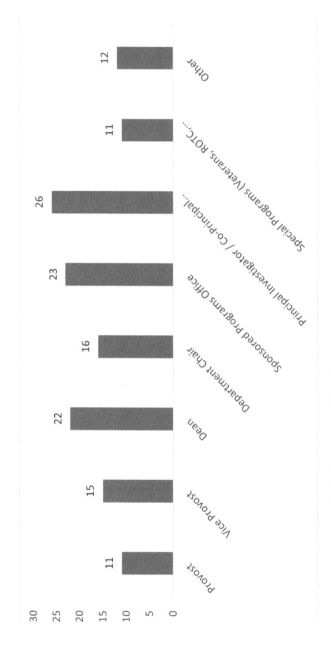

FIGURE 3-1 Engagement with the DOD, as reported by RFI respondents.
SOURCE: Committee-generated RFI.

Points of particular relevance to this study from RFI responses include the following:

- **Prioritization of research:** While 100 percent of respondents indicated that research is part of their institution's strategic plan, approximately one-third of respondents also indicated that research is not a high priority. This highlights the need to incentivize structures that support institutional engagement in research for the DOD to leverage significant unique capabilities available at these institutions.

- **Ability to conduct classified research:** Close to 80 percent of respondents indicated having access to classified infrastructure, either directly in-house or through established partnership agreements. This potentially indicates that lack of access to secure infrastructure is not an obstacle in engaging in DOD research. Other areas of investment/development—such as unclassified research infrastructure and specialized administrative, leadership, and management processes necessary for DOD research—are likely to lead to higher engagement.

- **Coordination of DOD strategy:** Connections to the DOD span multiple roles at an institution (provosts, vice presidents, etc.), but connections with individual principal investigators appear to be the most common. This data point, together with how institutions coordinate their research strategy, indicates that there may be a significant benefit from coordinating a DOD research strategy at multiple levels within institutions, including faculty leadership development programs specifically focused on DOD engagement such as the Tougaloo College Research and Development Foundation. Together with apparent access to classified infrastructure, such coordination has the potential to create a transition pathway from basic to applied research by leveraging currently untapped capabilities.

Several open-ended comments from respondents indicate opportunities for the DOD. One respondent noted, "Our institution has productive collaboration with DOD, and we are prepared to do more." Several noted their capabilities in such cutting-edge domains as directed energy, cybersecurity, and advanced materials. Suggestions included assigning DOD subject matter experts to MSIs full-time or on a rotational basis. The Army Research Laboratory Open Campus program could serve as a framework. This could jumpstart the needed external support and expertise to help faculty align their research more efficiently with DOD mandates and mission sets. Another cautioned, "Administrative and human capital systems are not adequate to support serious research in many instances" and pointed to the lack of defined professional development among staff and faculty to pursue in-depth research. One respondent suggested that the DOD include research professors as partners, which in turn supports students in the STEM workforce pipeline.

RECOMMENDATION 3-3: Inter-institutional collaborations among MSIs are an underutilized strategy to leverage unique perspectives, skills, and abilities to further the DOD research objectives. Frequently, no single institution possesses the necessary breadth of talent to broadly serve the DOD's research needs. Furthermore, under-resourced administrative staff often disincentivize MSI collaborations, especially when a well-resourced Primarily White Institutions R1 is poised to take the lead. To increase capacity development and engagement, the DOD should develop a funding program to support the creation of research consortia with an HBCU, TCU, HSI or other non-R1 MSI lead. The research consortia would focus on a clear area or project and include scholars from three or more MSIs. The committee is aware of the Research Institute for Tactical Autonomy, led by Howard University, an HBCU, and recommends that additional consortia be developed to address research projects of critical need to the DOD to facilitate the engagement of more MSIs. In the implementation of this funding program, the following factors should be included:
- **Support for developing consortia that fund R&D.**
- **Funding for at least 5 years for each consortium to support planning, execution, and evaluation activities.**
- **Support for consortia that exhibit intentional and equitable collaboration and mutually beneficial partnerships through strategies, including at least 6 months of pre-award communication, partnership agreements, and/or articulated resource and personnel sharing frameworks.**
- **Planning grants for prospective consortia to develop full proposals.**

- Supplements for institutional mentorship between MSIs and known performers to assist with the consortia's planning and implementation.

RECOMMENDATION 3-4: An under-resourced administrative infrastructure to secure, manage, and coordinate grants, contracts, and other opportunities is a significant barrier to engagement in the DOD and other federal agency opportunities. To increase the ability of under-resourced MSIs to adequately and effectively participate in opportunities, the DOD, with congressional support, should develop a funding program to develop administrative hubs. The administrative hubs would allow MSIs the option to coordinate through a professional organization that possesses the administrative expertise and resources necessary to support grant and contract acquisition and management (pre- and post-award). The hubs could also coordinate faculty and student participation in DOD opportunities, and communicate the current and evolving capabilities of member institutions. Additionally, these hubs would be used by three or more non-R1 MSIs that are regionally located or geographically close to facilitate coordination and mutual use and complications due to differences in administrative policies, complexities and protocols need to be built into use agreements. In the implementation of this program, the following factors should be included:

- Funding for at least 5 years to launch each hub and facilitate planning, execution, and evaluation.
- Support for lead organizations with clearly articulated missions relevant to MSIs who exhibit intentional development through strategies, such as the following:
  - Referencing at least 6 months of pre-award communication,
  - Partnership agreements with participating institutions,
  - An administrative capability track record, and
  - Clearly defined sustainability plans that demonstrate maintenance and long-term administrative support for participating institutions post-award.
- Planning grants for prospective hubs to develop full proposals.

REFERENCES

ACE (American Council on Education). 2023. Carnegie Classifications to make major changes in how colleges are grouped and recognized. https://www.acenet.edu/News-Room/Pages/Carnegie-Classifications-to-Make-Major-Changes.aspx.

Barton, P. 2002. Meeting the need for scientists, engineers, and an educated citizenry in a technological society. https://www.ets.org/research/policy_research_reports/publications/report/2002/cjuq.html.

Carnegie Classification of Institutions of Higher Education. 2024. About Carnegie Classification. https://carnegieclassifications.acenet.edu/.

Iḷisaġvik College. 2023. Annual report: Cooperation. https://indd.adobe.com/view/f9cb81fa-a634-49ee-9799-490984ad801b.

Minority Business Development Agency. 2021. Tribal colleges and universities, reservation entrepreneurship and business development. Minority Business Development Agency. U.S. Department of Commerce. https://www.mbda.gov/tribal-colleges-and-universities-reservation-entrepreneurship-and-business-development.

NASEM (National Academies of Sciences, Engineering, and Medicine). 2019. *Minority-serving institutions: America's underutilized resource for strengthening the STEM workforce.* Washington, DC: The National Academies Press. https://doi.org/10.17226/25257.

NASEM. 2024. *Building defense research capacity at historically black colleges and universities, tribal colleges and universities, and minority-serving institutions: Proceedings of three town halls.* Washington, DC: The National Academies Press. https://doi.org/10.17226/27511.

National Science Foundation. 2022a. Higher education research and development (HERD) survey 2021. National Center for Science and Engineering Statistics. https://ncses.nsf.gov/surveys/higher-education-research-development/2021#methodology.

National Science Foundation. 2022b. Survey of science and engineering research facilities 2021. National Center for Science and Engineering Statistics. https://ncses.nsf.gov/surveys/science-engineering-research-facilities/2021#methodology.

Tohono O'odham Community College. 2023. Annual report. https://tocc.edu/wp-content/uploads/2024/03/Final-for-Web-TOCC-AnRept2023-as-of-2.5.2024.pdf.

University of Alaska Anchorage. 2019. UAA ANSEP graduation study: UAA bachelor of science degrees awarded in engineering and other STEM majors comparisons (AY2000-2007 and AY2011-2018, by race and ethnicity). https://cdn.ansep.net/wp-content/uploads/2020/11/2019-UAA-ANSEP-Graduation-Study-04MAY19.pdf.

University of Alaska System. 2024. Alaska Native success initiative. Office of Race, Equity, Diversity, Inclusion, Success. https://www.alaska.edu/redis/ansi/.

U.S. Census Bureau. 2023. 2023 population projections for the nation by age, sex, race, Hispanic origin, and nativity. https://www.census.gov/newsroom/press-kits/2023/population-projections.html.

Zhang, R. 2024. *Building up research capacity at minority institutions: Report for the National Academy of Sciences.* Commissioned paper for the National Academies' Committee on the Development of a Plan to Promote Defense Research at Historically Black Colleges and Universities, Tribal Colleges and Universities, and Hispanic-Serving Institutions. https://nap.nationalacademies.org/catalog/27838.

4

Department of Defense and Other Federal Support for Research and Development

The federal government's investment in research and development (R&D) supports strengthening the nation's competitiveness and security. As noted in Chapter 1, this report focuses on defense-related research at the Department of Defense (DOD) as well as research supported by other agencies in service of the national security of the United States. This and other studies (e.g., NASEM, 2019, 2022) point to the competitive advantages of increasing the capacity of Historically Black Colleges and Universities (HBCUs), Tribal Colleges and Universities (TCUs), Hispanic-Serving Institutions (HSIs), and other minority-serving institutions (MSIs) to conduct defense-related research and train the next generation of scientists. Among the benefits to national and economic security are increases to the talent pool of U.S. citizens equipped to take on this work and to offer complementary areas of knowledge, innovation, and experience to the existing R&D ecosystem.

This chapter looks more closely at current and potential opportunities, primarily within the DOD but also at other agencies that perform defense-related research. In addition, the committee notes that while most defense-related research has focused on science, technology, engineering, and mathematics (STEM), the social sciences, humanities, and other disciplines have been shown to be important in addressing emerging mission needs that range from rapid adoption of autonomy to tackling the integrity of the information environment (NASEM, 2020). Moreover, some emerging national challenges, such as those related to environmental and societal impacts of new technologies, fall into the specific and unique expertise of many MSIs that have not traditionally engaged with the DOD. This recognition further calls for an acceleration of MSI participation in defense-related research.

DEPARTMENT OF DEFENSE

The DOD supports a well-defined pipeline of eight technology readiness levels mapped to contractual vehicles ranging from Basic Research (Budget Activity Code 6.1) to Software and Digital Technology Pipeline Programs (Budget Activity Code 6.8). Understanding the technology readiness levels and their impact on budgetary decision-making illustrates the existing national defense-related research infrastructure that can be leveraged for increased MSI engagement. In FY 2023, Congress appropriated $144 billion to this pipeline as a whole, known collectively as research, development, test, and evaluation (RDT&E). Within RDT&E, university science and technology (S&T) engagement typically occurs in the 6.1 through 6.3 parts of the pipeline: Basic Research (6.1), Applied Research (6.2), and, to a lesser extent, Advanced Technology Development (6.3). The FY 2023 budget for these three areas of research was $22.48 billion (DOD, 2023, 2024a), which represents a small increase over the past few years (Figure 4-1). Multiple entities within the DOD manage these funds. They include the Departments of the Air Force, Army, and Navy; offices within the Office of the Secretary of Defense; and defense agencies such as the Defense Advanced

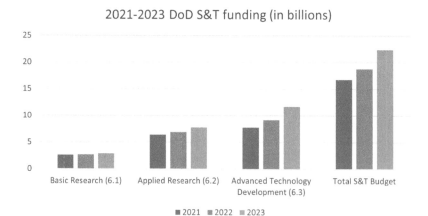

FIGURE 4-1 2021-2023 DOD S&T funding.
SOURCES: DOD, 2023, 2024a.

Research Projects Agency (DARPA) and the Defense Threat Reduction Agency (DTRA). (See NASEM, 2022, for further information.)

As discussed in greater detail below, despite the DOD efforts to explain and streamline the process, participants from institutions of all sizes shared with the committee their difficulty in navigating the system, given its scope and complexity. Universities that work successfully with the DOD must develop a unique set of administrative, infrastructure, and process capabilities, along with general awareness of mission needs. Even universities that have a record of funded research with other agencies such as the National Science Foundation (NSF) often require a different set of resources to engage at scale with the DOD. Working on the DOD research requires research infrastructure, different financial processes (e.g., related to contract rather than grant management), and, in some cases, specialized facilities.

The DOD has identified a pressing need to broaden its performer base given the scope of relevant challenges to be addressed, many of which require interdisciplinary expertise. Many national security challenges identified in guiding documents of the Department ranging from emerging technologies and how adversaries use them, to space exploration, to mitigating effects of climate change on national security, to supply chain resilience, to rapid adoption of artificial intelligence require bringing together the most diverse set of expertise possible. Making sure that the DOD is leveraging the unique research capabilities of MSIs, including HBCUs, TCUs, and HSIs, is vital to addressing those challenges. Social science research may offer a means of rapidly including HBCUs, TCUs, HSIs, and other MSIs in the DOD research portfolio (NASEM, 2020). Thus, the DOD could pursue initiatives that strengthen capacity for research across a broader performer base in areas of need for national security (e.g., STEM, social sciences, medicine, and related studies).

RECOMMENDATION 4-1: Engaging the breadth of research disciplines relevant to national security is necessary to fully explore opportunities and increase MSIs' engagement in defense-related R&D. Congress should create programs that increase the utilization of the full breadth of the DOD's research in non-engineering disciplines.

- **The DOD should further develop its research capacity by including and expanding funding to support the social sciences in its calls for proposals, focusing on the unique perspective MSIs bring to these fields. HBCUs, TCUs, and MSIs can provide rich contributions in the social sciences and other**

non-engineering-focused disciplines that are critical to DOD research.

Targeted Programs

Agency Perspectives

Within the DOD, the three military services, DARPA, DTRA, and other entities have programs that are either explicitly designed for MSIs or are particularly conducive to MSI participation. In addition, the locus for MSI engagement within the DOD is the Research and Education Program for Historically Black Colleges & Universities and Minority Institutions (MIs) within the Office of the Secretary of Defense. The office also serves as the DOD liaison to White House initiatives to promote educational equity, excellence, and economic opportunity.[1] While the office has made strong contributions, its budget of about $100 million represents only 0.56 percent of the S&T budget.

The committee heard presentations at its open sessions and reviewed materials to learn about DOD programs and goals related to engaging MSIs. A common thread was that MSIs are, and can become further, involved in DOD-funded research in priority areas, including in the 14 identified Critical Technology Areas or CTAs (see Chapter 3). The speakers detailed efforts to support research, faculty development, student training (from K-12 outreach through undergraduate to graduate/postdoc support), and infrastructure investment. The open sessions in November and December 2023 also provided a way for the committee to engage with the DOD and other organizations about where they see the opportunities and challenges for greater MSI involvement in defense-related research.

For example, the Navy's HBCU/MI program director stressed the value of personal engagement. Although he clarified that the program works carefully to ensure that prior history with the program does not influence funding decisions, he pointed out that (1) an important measure of success is engagement and number of connection points; (2) relevance to the DOD mission need is a key attribute of engaged institutions; (3)

---

[1] These include White House initiatives targeted to Black Americans (https:/sites.ed.gov/whblackinitiative/); Hispanic Americans (https://sites.ed.gov/hispanic-initiative/); Native Americans (https://sites.ed.gov/whiaiane/); and Asian American, Native Hawaiian, and Pacific Islander communities (https://www.whitehouse.gov/wp-content/uploads/2023/01/WHIAANHPI-2023-Report-to-the-President-FINAL.pdf).

in-person engagements are critical to success, but resource limitations make those engagements difficult to scale; and (4) regular engagement leads to more productive, mutually beneficial relationships and addressing of DOD mission needs.

The Director of Social Sciences for the Office of the Under Secretary of Defense for Research and Engineering discussed the Minerva Research Initiative.[2] He observed that while interdisciplinary social science research and collaborations are encouraged, the office does not have specific programs focused on HBCUs, TCUs, or other MSIs. Possible development of such programs could be beneficial to the DOD and leverage advanced research capabilities available at those institutions.

The Air Force Office of Scientific Research program manager for HBCUs and MSIs highlighted the need for capacity building along with supporting faculty and researcher pathways through engagements with the DOD. The Air Force representatives highlighted programs ranging from grants to Small Business Innovation Research and Small Business Technology Transfer in support of small businesses.

The technical engagement program manager at DTRA highlighted the importance of understanding broad research capabilities across HBCUs and MSIs. His focus was on workforce development and opportunities for engaging with DTRA-relevant programs in chemical, biological, radiological, and nuclear threats.

A representative from DARPA discussed several opportunities, including DARPAConnect, which is focused on broadening institutional participation in DARPA programs. DARPA also has engagement, outreach, and education programs focused on institutions that may not have had previous engagement with the agency.

Overall, these presentations highlighted the following:

- The need for a better understanding of key institutional research strengths for MSIs that do not typically engage with the DOD.
- The importance of addressing DOD's mission needs in research and engineering with a broad a set of capabilities available nationally.
- The critical role of in-person engagement and barriers to scaling that approach.

---

[2] For more information on the Minerva Research Initiative, see https://minerva.defense.gov/.

- The challenge of building and sustaining research infrastructure and the management of teaching loads at HBCUs, TCUs, HSIs, and other MSIs.

Examples of Programs for MSIs

Through presentations at the open sessions, the 2023 Town Halls (NASEM, 2024), and their own experience, committee members reviewed a variety of programs targeted at MSIs. The information below is not meant to be exhaustive but instead offers examples of initiatives related to research, faculty, student, and infrastructure support, some of which could be expanded or replicated in other parts of the Department.

Research Grants: In FY 2023, the HBCU/MI program funded 82 researchers for 4-year grants totaling $61.7 million. A supplemental program sponsored by the Office of Naval Research (ONR) funded an additional $27 million to HBCUs to conduct research in relevant CTAs.[3] The U.S. Army Combat Capabilities Development Command Army Research Laboratory (ARL) administers the Research and Education Program for HBCUs/MIs on behalf of the Office of the Under Secretary of Defense for Research and Engineering, with collaboration opportunities available to broader academia as well as opportunities targeted to HBCUs/MIs.[4] The Department of the Navy's HBCU/MI program supports the participation of underrepresented institutions in navy-relevant RDT&E programs and activities. In addition to core basic and applied research programs executed by ONR program officers and research performed at naval laboratories, ONR sponsors research programs performed by academic research institutions, including the Defense University Research Instrumentation Program (DURIP).

Faculty Support: The DOD HBCU/MI Faculty Fellowship Program aims to strengthen the collaboration between the DOD and STEM faculty affiliated with HBCUs and other MSIs.[5] Other opportunities for faculty under

---

[3] For more information, see https://dodhbcumiopportunities.com/. For the ONR Supplemental Awards, see https://www.cto.mil/27mil-investment-hbcu/.

[4] For more information on general opportunities, see https://arl.devcom.army.mil/collaborate-with-us/audience/academia/. For opportunities for HBCUs/MIs, see https://arl.devcom.army.mil/collaborate-with-us/audience/hbcu-mi/.

[5] For more information, see https://orau.org/usre/.

the Office of Basic Research include the Vannevar Bush Faculty Fellowship; Minerva Research Initiative in collaboration with the U.S. Institute of Peace; and the Academic Research Security initiatives with more than 130 opportunities including development, fellowships, and internships.[6] Young Investigator programs are also administered by the Navy, Air Force, and DARPA; these are not targeted to MSIs or minority investigators at non-MSIs.[7]

Student Support: The DOD HBCU/MI Summer Research Internship Program aims to increase the number of minority scientists and engineers throughout the DOD.[8] The DOD maintains an overarching program called DOD STEM, which highlights collaboration between the DOD (including all branches/other federal agencies) and those involved in STEM K-12, undergraduate/graduate, and early career programs across the country. It offers a database of current STEM program, internship, and scholarship opportunities across the country.[9] The Science, Mathematics, and Research for Transformation (SMART) program offers scholarships and stipends to students, who then commit to working with the DOD as civilian employees.[10]

Infrastructure Support: The Office of the Under Secretary of Defense for Research and Engineering provides technical assistance workshops as part of a series of training and educational activities intended to provide program, process, and funding opportunities and information to MSIs. The workshops focus on both DOD funding opportunities and best practices in writing effective technical proposals. Representatives from the Office of the Secretary of Defense, Army, Navy, Air Force, and other federal agencies present funding opportunity information along with insights on writing competitive proposals in response to Broad Agency Announcements and other funding opportunities. The Defense Innovation Marketplace provides

---

[6] For more information, see https://DODhbcumiopportunities.com/.

[7] For information on the ONR Young Investigator Program, see https://www.nrc.navy.mil/education-outreach/sponsored-research/yip. For the Air Force Research Laboratory Young Investigator Program, see https://afresearchlab.com/. For the DARPA Young Faculty Award, see https://www.darpa.mil/work-with-us/for-universities/young-faculty-award.

[8] For more information, see https://DODhbcumiinternship.com/.

[9] For more information, see https://DODstem.us/.

[10] For more information on SMART, see https://www.smartscholarship.org/smart.

opportunities such as Technology Interchange Meetings and Communities of Interest.[11]

RECOMMENDATION 4-2: Beginning in FY2026, the DOD Under Secretary of Defense for Research and Engineering should collect and publish data annually that measure the efficacy of existing outreach programs targeting MSIs, and share lessons learned with DOD agencies to accelerate the dissemination of best practices.

- This report should include a longitudinal analysis to provide evidence of successful engagement and impact. Potential metrics should include the following:
  - ○ Number of MSIs engaged quarterly,
  - ○ Data on personnel interacted with (investigators, administrators, students),
  - ○ Institution type,
  - ○ Hours and type of engagement,
  - ○ Number of applications received and time to successful award, and
  - ○ Measurement of research infrastructure growth among awardees (instrumentation, research-engaged faculty, administration support, etc.).

Metrics collected should be used to set a baseline for improvement of how the DOD engages with MSIs. They should be assessed annually to direct resources and engagement activities toward increased participation in DOD R&D.

- The DOD Under Secretary of Defense for Research and Engineering should administer new outreach programs that do the following:
  - ○ Create and deploy a DOD liaison to HBCUs, TCUs, and MSIs to translate DOD interests to the university and university capabilities and interests to the DOD.
  - ○ Place scientists and engineers from local military labs at MSIs to teach STEM courses and provide course load relief for investigators pursuing and conducting defense-related research, as referenced in Chapter 3. A potential framework

---

[11] For more information, see https://defenseinnovationmarketplace.dtic.mil/about/. For the Communities of Interest, see https://defenseinnovationmarketplace.dtic.mil/communities-of-interest/. For business opportunities, see https://defenseinnovationmarketplace.dtic.mil/business-opportunities/.

could be the use of the Intergovernmental Personnel Act Mobility Program.[12]
- The DOD Under Secretary of Defense for Research and Engineering should expand existing outreach programs so that HBCU, TCU, and MSI employees are eligible for sabbaticals to gain R&D experience with DOD acquisition and operations organizations.

These new outreach programs will allow for increased awareness and provide teaching load relief to HBCU, TCU, and MSI faculty conducting DOD R&D. In doing so, however, DOD's HBCU/MI programs should address institutions' unique contexts and needs rather than group HBCU, TCU, HSI, and other MSI engagements. A one-size-fits-all approach decreases the successful engagement of MSIs, given the diversity of needs, challenges, engagement, and opportunities within and across MSIs. To plan and implement more granular interventions, the DOD should undertake robust comment periods, listening sessions, and dialogue with institutions and their supporting communities to develop engagement frameworks tailored to each MSI type to increase the Department's success in its engagement with MSIs and relationship development activities. This approach is both in the strategic interest of the DOD and helps support global competitiveness, national security, and historic disparities.

Committee Analysis of DOD Opportunities

As noted above, a concern was expressed during the site visits and in other feedback from MSIs in which faculty researchers noted the complexity of the application process as a barrier to engaging with the DOD for research funding opportunities. Accepting that success rates are not high in any proposal-based award system, it is clear that there are advantages in having research officers and faculty who are well versed in how to interpret and respond to Requests for Proposals (RFPs) and who have the time and resources to develop proposals.

In this analysis, five active DOD RFPs/funding opportunity announcements (FOAs) were randomly selected from grants.gov, which had a total of 67 active RFPs/FOAs available for review at the time of the analysis. A

---

[12] For more information, see https://www.doi.gov/pmb/hr/ipa-mobility-program.

content analysis followed by a thematic analysis were used to review the selected RFPs/FOAs.

Content analysis determined if each DOD RFP/FOA had the same core structures: (1) Program Overview, (2) Eligibility, (3) Submission Information, (4) Application Detail, and (5) Award Information (Table 4-1).

A thematic analysis of the content revealed several implications and learnings:

- **No uniform RFP/FOA format.** Unlike agencies such as the National Institutes of Health (NIH) or NSF, there is no standard or uniformity to the design or order of information across the DOD RFPs/FOAs. This is true even within divisions; for example, W911NF-19-S-0001 and W911NF-19-S-0004, both supported by the Department of the Army Materiel Command, differed in font and design style and level of detail in each section (Table 4-2). The lack of standardization in the information provided in some RFPs/FOAs may contribute to challenges with accessibility for some RFPs/FOAs.

- **Difference in evaluative criteria or expectations.** For example, W911NF-19-S-0013 provides clear objectives to which applicants can respond, but other RFPs/FOAs do not include specific references to objectives, despite outlining criteria related to scientific merit, impact on the DOD mission, and innovation/relevance.

- **Inconsistent points of contact.** Not all RFPs/FOAs had a designated point of contact. In some cases, a general program email was provided, while others did not include this information. In FOA-RVK-2019-001, for example, no email was provided, despite the instructions using the following language:

  > For administrative issues regarding this FOA, contact the grants specialist at the email address identified above. For technical issues regarding this FOA, please contact the Primary Technical POC at the email address identified above. All questions must be received in writing via email with the reference line referring to this notice (FOA-RVK-2019-0001).

- **Inconsistency in feedback procedures**. Some RFPs/FOAs state that feedback will only be provided to funded proposals. If feedback is only provided to competitive proposals, those applicants who did not receive funding will be at a disadvantage as they lack insight into steps they can take to improve a future submission.

Overall, the variation and diversity across DOD RFPs/FOAs in terms of their construction and submission processes may contribute to lower submission rates by MSIs who may lack the resources to navigate the DOD system. Akin to national standardized assessments like those used for collegiate or graduate school admission, if such tools change their structure each year, or differ by state, then it would systematically disadvantage a number of individuals. Such is the case with varying RFP formats and structures across the DOD. Further providing increased engagement of MSI researchers within review panels will help address potential implicit bias.

University Affiliated Research Centers and Federally Funded Research and Development Centers

The DOD has also created a network of 15 University Affiliated Research Centers (UARCs) and 10 Federally Funded Research and Development Centers (FFRDCs) (Tables 4-3 and 4-4). These centers vary in size with core competencies aligned to specific DOD needs. A high priority is placed on acquiring UARC and FFRDC unique technical expertise in areas in which the DOD cannot attract and retain personnel in sufficient depth and numbers on its own. The advantage to the UARC/FFRDC is the strong relationship developed with the DOD that can lead to substantial and sustainable investments.

A UARC is a nonprofit research organization within a university or college that provides or maintains essential DOD engineering, research, and/or development capabilities. Each UARC has core competencies in leading-edge research, development, or engineering that are tailored to meet the needs of the DOD. UARCs provide the DOD support in early S&T programs (6.1 and 6.2 research) as well as in advanced technical development, advanced component development, and prototype engineering programs (6.3 and 6.4) (DOD, 2024b).

The ongoing need for each UARC is evaluated every 5 years. Each UARC is required to operate in the public interest and conduct its business in a manner befitting its special relationship with the government. This

TABLE 4-1 Analysis of Five Randomly Selected DOD RFPs/FOAs

RFP/FOA #	Overview Included	Eligibility Clear	Process for Applying	Description of Criteria	Miscellaneous
BROAD AGENCY ANNOUNCEMENT (BAA) for Extramural Biomedical Research and Development (W81XWH-18-S-SOC1, Modified-004)	X	Award mechanism confusing; "The USAMRAA will negotiate the award types consisting of either contracts, grants or cooperative agreements for proposals/ applications selected for funding."	"(1) pre-proposal/pre-application submission through eBRAP (https://eBRAP.org/) and (2) full proposal/application submission through Grants.gov or eBRAP, depending on the type of application being submitted." "A Proposal/Application will not be accepted unless the PI has received an invitation to submit."	"Pre-Proposal/Pre-Application Narrative (6-page limit):… Problem to Be Studied, Theoretical Rationale, Scientific Methods, and Design (Background/ Rationale, Hypothesis/ Objective and Specific Aims, Approach/ Methodology); Significance, Relevance, and Innovation of the Proposed Effort (Significance and Relevance, Innovation); Proposed Study Design/Plan; Military Impact; Personnel and Facilities; Open Source/ License/Architecture"	"PIs will be notified as to whether or not they are invited to submit full proposals/ applications; however, they will not receive feedback (e.g., a critique of strengths and weaknesses) on their pre-proposals/ pre-applications."

continued

| ARL Strengthening Teamwork for Robust Operations in Novel Groups (STRONG) (W911NF-19-S-0001, amendment 9) | X | Table of contents does not align with the RFP/FOA | Thorough for Grants.gov steps: "Project Summary/ Abstract, Project Narrative (Chapter 1: Technical Component- Proposed Effort (approximately 4 pages, Proposed Innovation Summit Series Participation and Collaboration Development (approximately 1 pages); Chapter 2: Cost Component; Bibliography and Reference Cite; Facilities and Other Resources; Equipment; Data Management Plan" | "Pre-Proposal/Pre-Application Supporting Documentation" "Thorough—narrative description" "Factor 1: Scientific Merit and Relevance Factor 2: Experience and Qualifications of Scientific Staff and Junior Investigator Development Factor 3: Collaboration/ Ecosystem support Factor 4: Cost" | "Applicants will receive feedback regarding their proposal ONLY IF IT IS SELECTED FOR AWARD." RFP/FOA thorough Review and Selection Process |

TABLE 4-1 Continued

RFP/FOA #	Overview Included	Eligibility Clear	Process for Applying	Description of Criteria	Miscellaneous
AFRL RV-RD Assistance Instruments Announcement –AFRL Space Vehicles (RV) and Directed Energy (RD) University Assistance Instruments (FOA-RVK-2019-0001)	X	Not identified as Eligibility— "GENERAL INFORMATION: Only U.S./U.S. territory educational institutions are eligible to submit proposals in response to this notice"	Project Narrative, "Identify and describe how the effort will provide assistance that will stimulate or support a public purpose; (b) Project Narrative - Statement of Work; (c) Project Narrative - Research Effort; (d) Project Narrative - Principal Investigator (PI) Time; (e) Project Narrative – Facilities; (f) Project Narrative – Special Test Equipment; (g) Project Narrative – Equipment"	Not thorough.... "The recipient shall submit a proposal describing the proposed research project's (1) objective, (2) general approach, (3) public purpose in accordance with 32 CFR § 22.205, and 22.215 and (4) impact on Department of Defense (DOD) mission. The proposal shall also contain any unique capabilities or experience you may have (e.g., U.S. Air Force, DOD, or other Federal laboratory)."	Point of contact (POC) present in RFP/FOA

continued

Research and Education Program for Historically Black Colleges and Universities/Minority-Serving Institutions ((FOA) W911NF-19-S-0013 Amendment 02)	X synopsis vs. overview	Must refer to original 2019 FOA	White paper: "TECHNICAL CONTENT (not to exceed five pages), ADDENDUM (not to exceed one page)"	"ARL staff will perform an initial review of its scientific merit and potential contribution to the Army mission, and also determine if funds are expected to be available for the effort.	RFP/FOA has objectives
		"The ACC-APG RTP Division has the authority to award a variety of instruments on behalf of CCDC ARL. Anticipated awards under this FOA include grants and cooperative agreements"	"Scientific Division(s) or Directorate(s), Technical Area(s)/Program Manager, The research to be undertaken in a level of detail that fully addresses the objectives of the research and approaches to be used, and the relationship of the project to the state of knowledge in the field and to any related work at the institution or elsewhere. vi. The anticipated results and how the project relates to the research interests of the Agency(ies).	Proposals not considered having sufficient scientific merit or relevance to the Army's needs, or those in areas for which funds are not expected to be available, may not receive further review....Each proposal will be evaluated based on the evaluation criteria in accordance with BAA W911NF-19-	"Identified Specific Actions of the Senior/ Key Personnel" (high/Moderate/Low ranking) rubric

TABLE 4-1 Continued

RFP/FOA #	Overview Included	Eligibility Clear	Process for Applying	Description of Criteria	Miscellaneous
			vii. The facilities and equipment available for performing the proposed research. viii. The involvement of undergraduate and/or graduate students in the research project and associated research-related education is encouraged. Program funds may be requested for scholarships and fellowships pursuant to 10 U.S.C. 2362. The involvement of students in the research project is critical to achieving program objectives."	S-0013. Each evaluated proposal will receive a recommendation of "select" or "do not select" as supported by the evaluation."	

| BROAD AGENCY ANNOUNCEMENT (BAA) FOR BASIC AND APPLIED RESEARCH (W911QY-20-R-0022) | X | "Who may submit…" "Types of instrumentation… Combat Capabilities Development Command (CCDC), Natick Contracting Division has the authority to award procurement contracts, cooperative agreements, and grants, and reserves the right to use the type of instrument most appropriate for the effort proposed." | "Concept papers may not exceed 5 single-sided 8 ½ x 11 inch typed pages (including charts, photographs, graphs, etc.) and shall include the following: (1) A brief technical explanation of the proposed effort that addresses the major research thrust, the research goals and deliverables, a proposed approach to achieve these goals and deliverables, and military relevancy. (2) A brief 'management' description outlining key personnel and experience. (3) Any past performance the contractor has with similar research efforts. (4) An estimated cost/price and performance schedule for the work." | Part I - Technical Section Part II - Management Section Part III - Cost/Price Section Part IV - Past Performance Section Part V – Subcontracting & Small Business Participation Part VI - Contractor Representations and Certifications Part VII - Contractor Statement of Work | The clearest table of contents of all the RFPs. Additional paperwork: "contractor manpower reporting requirements"; "Executive compensation reporting"; "Government furnished Property request" |

SOURCE: Committee-generated.

TABLE 4-2 Comparison of Proposal Requirements for Two DOD RFPs/FOAs

	W911NF-19-S-0001	W911NF-19-S-0004
Special Notes		Format of announcement chart
Table of Contents	Text without subheadings	Outlined Chart with subheading text
Program Description	Background, Cycle Structure, Deliverables, Updates	16 areas of interest
Award Information	Definition of funding types	List of federal regulations
Eligibility	3 sections (applicant, cost sharing, other)	2 sections (applicant & cost sharing)
Submission Information	11 sections across 11 pages	8 sections across 16 pages
Application Review Information	3 sections (criteria, review & selection process, recipient qualifications across 2 pages)	3 sections (criteria, review & selection process, recipient qualifications across 10 pages to include definitions, Army Research Risk Assessment Program (ARRP) rubric, and required actions by applicants)
Award Administration	5 sections over 4 pages	3 sections over 14 pages
Agency Contact	Paragraph directions, general email	4 enumerated directions, general email
Other Information	Human Subjects Directions	Example of Cost Proposal Budget Narrative Example of Budget Narrative for Grant and Cooperative Agreement Proposal Appendix with Acronyms

SOURCE: Committee-generated.

TABLE 4-3 DOD University Affiliated Research Centers

DOD UARC	University	Primary Sponsor	Founded
Georgia Tech Research Institute	Georgia Institute of Technology	Army	1995
Institute for Soldier Nanotechnologies	Massachusetts Institute of Technology	Army	2002
Institute for Collaborative Biotechnologies	University of California, Santa Barbara	Army	2003
Institute for Creative Technologies	University of Southern California	Army	1999
Applied Physics Laboratory	The Johns Hopkins University	Navy	1942
Applied Research Laboratory	Penn State University	Navy	1945
Applied Research Laboratory	University of Hawaii	Navy	2008
Applied Research Laboratories	University of Texas at Austin	Navy	1945
Applied Physics Laboratory	University of Washington	Navy	1943
Space Dynamics Laboratory	Utah State University	Missile Defense Agency (MDA)	1996
Systems Engineering Research Center	Stevens Institute of Technology	USD(R&E)/ ADF(MC)	2008
Applied Research Laboratory for Intelligence & Security	University of Maryland, College Park	USD(I)	2017
National Strategic Research Institute	University of Nebraska	STRATCOM	2012
Geophysical Detection of Nuclear Proliferation	University of Alaska	DASD(TRAC)	2018
Research Institute for Tactical Autonomy	Howard University	USAF	2023

SOURCE: Committee-generated.

TABLE 4-4 DOD Federally Funded Research and Development Centers

DOD FFRDCs	Primary Sponsor	Founded
Study & Analysis		
Center for Naval Analyses	Navy (ASN(RDA))	1942
Institute for Defense Analyses (IDA) -Studies and Analyses	USD(A&S)	1956
RAND – Arroyo Center	HQDA G-8/PAE	1982
RAND – National Defense Research Institute (NDRI)	USD(A&S)	1984
RAND – Project Air Force	Air Force (SAF/AQ)	1948
Systems Engineering & Integration		
Aerospace Corporation	Air Force (SAF/AQ)	1961
MITRE Corporation – National Security Engineering Center (NSEC)	USD(R&E) / ASD(S&T)	1958
Research & Development Laboratories		
Institute for Defense Analyses (IDA) – Communications & Computing	National Security Agency	1959
Massachusetts Institute of Technology— Lincoln Laboratory (MIT/LL)	USD(R&E) / ASD(S&T)	1951
Software Engineering Institute (SEI)	USD(R&E) / ASD(S&T)	1984

SOURCE: Department of Defense Research and Engineering Enterprise. Federally Funded Research and Development Centers (FFRDC) and University Affiliated Research Centers (UARC). https://rt.cto.mil/ffrdc-uarc/.

includes operating under a comprehensive policy limiting its operations to be free from conflicts of interest. Generally, UARCs may not compete against industry in response to competitive RFPs for development or production contracts. They are required to maintain a long-term strategic relationship with the DOD in a manner that provides the following:

- Responsiveness to evolving sponsors' requirements.
- Comprehensive knowledge of sponsors' requirements and problems.
- Broad access to information, including proprietary data.
- Broad corporate knowledge.
- Independence and objectivity.
- Quick response capability.
- Current operational experience.
- Freedom from real and/or perceived conflicts of interest.

The present set of 15 DOD UARCs (Table 4-3) includes one managed by an HBCU. Other MSIs have been involved in UARCs but generally in a small role. There is potential for more substantive involvement of MSIs when expertise is aligned with the mission of the UARC. For example, in a presentation to the committee, the director of the UARC at the University of Alaska expressed a willingness to increase engagement with MSIs with geoscience faculty.

FFRDCs are independent, nonprofit research organizations that are established and funded to meet specific long-term engineering, research, development, or other analytic DOD needs that cannot be met as effectively by government or industry resources. FFRDCs are operated and managed by nonprofit corporations; one is affiliated with the university (Massachusetts Institute of Technology/Lincoln Labs). FFRDCs are required to operate in the public interest and conduct business in a manner befitting their special relationship with the government, including a comprehensive conflict of interest policy. Each FFRDC is assigned a primary sponsor responsible for implementing the DOD's policies and procedures, assessing its performance, maintaining the tenets of the sponsoring agreement, conducting a comprehensive review every 5 years, and approving all work done by the center (DOD, 2024b). The present set of 10 FFRDCs is listed in Table 4-4.

Leaders from several UARCs and FFRDCs spoke with the committee at its open sessions. Common themes from these conversations were that centers did the following:

- Built up unique facilities, capabilities, and experiences that meet specific needs of the DOD.
- Emphasized strong and nearly singular organizational alignment with U.S. defense and national security priorities.
- Sought to increase diversity in their S&T workforce including graduates of HBCUs, HSIs, and TCUs.
- Developed, to greater or lesser extents, research collaborations and personnel exchanges with a broad set of universities to foster defense-related research across institutions, including engagement with HBCUs, HSIs, and TCUs.
- Engaged with the National Society of Black Engineers, Society of Hispanic Professional Engineers, Advancing Minorities, Interest in Engineers, and other organizations to accelerate the growth of a diverse workforce into S&T education and career paths.

Through its present set of UARCs and FFRDCs, the DOD has a research network that spans most of the United States (Figures 4-2 and 4-3). Many UARCs and FFRDCs are located relatively close to MSIs. While most TCUs are not geographically close to existing UARCs, there may be an opportunity for the DOD to take advantage of this proximity for greater engagement by UARCs and FFRDCs with MSIs.

In addition, the DOD consistently collects metrics on the performance of its UARCs and FFRDCs in terms of small and disadvantaged business engagement. The committee believes it would be instructive to collect similar data regarding the research connectivity between DOD UARCs, FFRDCs, and the HBCUs, TCUs, HSIs, and other MSIs in their region. Furthermore, the DOD, UARCs and FFRDCs will need to assess the unique opportunities, challenges, and risks of developing these partnerships in order to develop sustainable relationships.

RECOMMENDATION 4-3: The DOD should allocate resources to assess the potential for regional connectivity and partnerships between existing DOD labs, UARCs, and FFRDCs, and local or regional HBCUs, TCUs, and MSIs. This assessment should include collecting metrics on existing and potential research collaborations between these entities.

- **Based on this assessment described above, the DOD should provide guidance to DOD labs, UARCs, and FFRDCs about how to support and expand collaborative R&D with MSIs within proximity or sharing similar research foci.**

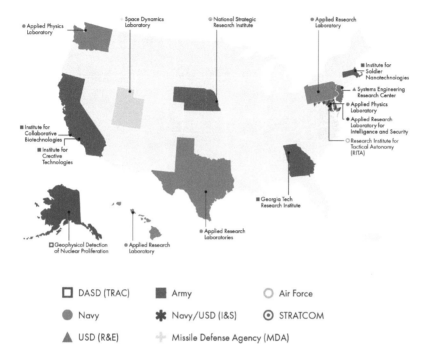

FIGURE 4-2 U.S. distribution of UARCs.
SOURCE: Defense Innovation Marketplace, https://defenseinnovationmarketplace.
dtic.mil/ffrdcs-uarcs.

- **The DOD should develop a pilot funding opportunity that allows MSI investigators to develop research projects with investigators at DOD labs, UARCs, and FFRDCs. Awards should include MSI investigators as lead investigators, co-investigators, or lead contractors.**

OTHER AGENCY MODELS AND OPPORTUNITIES

Defense-related research is sponsored not only by the DOD but also by other federal agencies. It includes basic and applied research that supports the national security of the United States and is useful to DOD force readiness. In addition to the DOD, federal agencies, such as NIH, NSF, National Aeronautics and Space Administration (NASA), Environmental Protection Agency, and Department of Energy (DOE), sponsor research

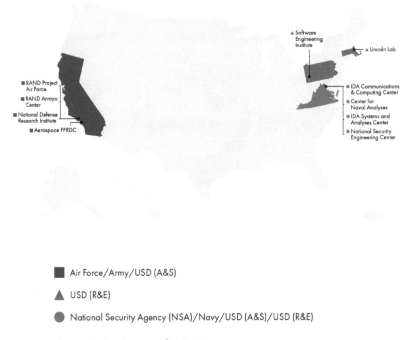

FIGURE 4-3 U.S. distribution of FFRDCs.
SOURCE: Emerging Technology Policy Careers, the Horizon Institute for Public Service, https://emergingtechpolicy.org/institutions/national-labs-and-ffrdcs/#:~:-text=Overview%20of%20the%20national%20labs%20today,-Beyond%20the%20 nuclear.

and scholarship at HBCUs, HSIs, and TCUs in domains useful to national security. Examples include, but are not limited to, studies in materials science, microbiology, toxicology, marine science, and oceanography.

Other federal agencies recognize the need to provide funding that precipitates new applications in R&D and a more diverse, STEM-capable workforce. These agencies have developed and administered programs throughout their history in an effort to increase representation and engagement of under-resourced and underinvested institutions and communities. A long-standing example can be found in NSF's proposal criteria included as part of its Broadening Participation Portfolio (NSF, 2011; James and Singer, 2016). Applicants must show how their proposed research will benefit society and contribute to the achievements in specific, desired societal impacts. While imperfect and drawing criticism from NSF's funded community (e.g., Tretkoff, 2007), this requirement signals to current and future grantees, grant reviewers, and staff that increasing participation from under-resourced institutions and communities is important to the science, engineering, and innovation ecosystem and to the nation. NSF's Broadening Participation Portfolio seeks to broaden the gender, racial, ethnic, and geographic diversity among fund awardees.

This level of intentionality manifests across federal science agencies with programs that offer support to faculty and trainees; target funding for capacity, both physical and administrative; and increase opportunities for the development of institutional partnerships. The committee hosted representatives from several science funding agencies during open sessions to better understand the breadth of interventions used across the federal government. In addition, the committee drew on discussions during the Town Hall series referenced in Chapters 1 and 3 (NASEM, 2024). As in the case of looking at DOD programs, the summary below is not an exhaustive view of every program across the federal government. Instead, the summary highlights examples of how other federal agencies have increased engagement with underinvested institutions that may inform the DOD as it considers how to develop or reconfigure its own programs.

Individual Support

The development of funding mechanisms that provide individual researchers and students with support to pursue degrees and advance areas of national need in STEM has long been a practice at federal funding agencies. The NSF Graduate Research Fellowship, which provides 3 years of funding for research-focused master's and doctoral students, is an integral mechanism for supporting the training of a generation of future innovators and contributors to U.S. R&D (NSF, 2024). At NIH, the National Institute of General Medical Sciences (NIGMS) Maximizing Opportunities for Scientific and Academic Independent Careers (MOSAIC) program provides a framework to support the successful transition of postdoctoral scholars to faculty positions. Through the MOSAIC program, individuals receive independent support. Additionally, organizations, such as scientific societies, can receive funding to develop networks that offer mentoring, networking, and career development across relevant research fields (NIH, 2024b). The NIGMS Maximizing Investigators' Research Award (MIRA) provides targeted funding for established and new investigators with a specific funding mechanism for early-stage investigators (NIH, 2024a). MIRA is designed to provide stable funding over a 5-year period to investigators pursuing research within the NIGMS mission to develop and support their labs. MIRA is broken out into tracks for established, new, and early career investigators to help address competition among different career levels while maintaining support for investigators across their careers. This stability and tailored funding addresses the needs of investigators throughout their careers to ensure that NIGMS is not only launching the next generation of researchers but also retaining them in the research enterprise for sustained advancement and contribution to the NIGMS R&D portfolio.

Findings:
- The R&D workforce can be expanded and strengthened through synergistic programs that create continuous funding sources for trainees (undergraduate, graduate, postdoctoral) and faculty researchers, with a specific target for MSIs. As an example, NIH allots funding for individual trainees or faculty that provides flexibility and independence. This funding covers periods of time for stability at the trainee level (~3 years) and for the establishment of a research lab (5+ years).
- Programs that are decoupled across career levels and previous engagement with an agency's funding can support early, mid-, established, and new researchers.

Capacity Building

A diverse range of potential interventions can increase the capacity of MSIs to participate in federal R&D, defense-related or otherwise. Legislation, such as the CHIPS and Science Act, the DOE Science for the Future Act, FY22 and FY23 National Defense Authorization Acts, and others, detail the importance of increasing the capacity of underinvested and under-resourced institutions to contribute to the nation's workforce, innovation ecosystem, competitiveness, and national security (U.S. Congress, 2021, 2022a, 2022b). Among the programs administered across the federal government, several frameworks, if appropriated or incorporated into existing programmatic structures, could increase the ability of MSIs to be significant contributors to DOD's R&D ecosystem.

For example, NASA's Science Mission Directorate (SMD) Bridge Program addresses capacity development of underinvested institutions that have not historically been a part of its performer base in an intentional and structured way (NASA, 2024). The SMD Bridge Program is organized across two tracks: seed grants and full Bridge funding. Seed grants are budgeted for 2 years of support at up to $300,000. They are designed to build and strengthen partnerships between targeted institutions and develop the foundation necessary for institutions to successfully compete for major NASA grants and full Bridge Program funding.

Like the NIGMS MIRA program mentioned in the previous section, the SMD Bridge Program is designed to develop sustainable research programs and relationships to advance the NASA mission directorate's five science divisions. Unlike MIRA, however, the SMD Bridge Program gears its funding toward institutions historically under-resourced by NASA, which include the breadth of MSIs and primarily undergraduate institutions (PUIs). It seeks to develop lasting collaborations between NASA's existing infrastructure, such as its centers, labs, and R1 institution performers, and MSIs. An integral component of the SMD Bridge Program is an ongoing assessment and adjustment of what is effective and not effective. Throughout the creation and administration of the funding opportunity, regular community input is solicited and incorporated through virtual workshops to integrate the target community's perspective into each iteration of the funding opportunity. Proposals are submitted by faculty at an MSI/PUI and co-written with a NASA partner with paid research positions for students on topics relevant to NASA's divisions and an emphasis on sustainability and mentorship. To add more flexibility to the types of projects that institutions can pursue, the SMD Bridge Program tiers its funding for bridge awards at small (<$70,000), medium (<$150,000), and large or key proposals (<$500,000), with the large or key proposals having a maximum budget of $2 million per year and required to incorporate the development of a consortium that serves multiple MSIs/PUIs.

The DOE's Reaching a New Energy Sciences Workforce (RENEW) and Funding for Accelerated, Inclusive Research (FAIR) programs were also developed with a significant amount of community input to ensure that the programs' frameworks adequately approach addressing historical barriers to engagement in the DOE's research ecosystem. These programs provide priority for underinvested institutions and institutions that have received no prior funding from DOE's Office of Science (U.S. Department of Energy, 2023). RENEW is intended to provide direct support for teaching staff, administration, instrumentation, and students (U.S. Department of Energy, n.d.). FAIR is geared toward building research programs at MSIs and emerging research institutions (U.S. Federal Register 42 USC § 18901(5)).

Similar to NASA's SMD Bridge, FAIR provides support for underinvested institutions to develop sustainable research partnerships between target institutions, national labs, and Office of Science user facilities.

Both NASA and DOE have delineated an intentional effort to address implicit bias and diversity in grant reviews and reviewers. Reviewers are given explicit direction and orientation on implicit bias awareness and mitigation strategies to support a more comprehensive and fair evaluation of institutions that either have never been a part of the funded community or do not align with assumptions of what a normal performer could be.

NSF's Growing Research Access for Nationally Transformative Equity and Diversity (GRANTED) addresses another component of capacity development highlighted in the National Academies' 2022 study, specifically a strong institutional research and contract base and ancillary services. GRANTED funding is geared toward providing support for the development of best practices and processes for institutional grant administration, human capital, and the translation of best practices to practical applications. Recognizing that there is no one-size-fits-all mechanism for increasing capacity, GRANTED is designed to collect a comprehensive scope of the diversity of interventions necessary for increasing capacity at non-R1 institutions and use that information for cross-pollination of ideas and the development of new programs to address critical needs across institutions.

Through the Department of Commerce, the Economic Development Administration Regional Technology Innovation Hub (Tech Hub) program may serve as a framework for pooling DOD's resources while supporting infrastructure needs of MSIs. Strategic development grants are used to assess the effectiveness of a regional hub to support cross-sectoral consortia that collaborate toward an identified technology focus. An analogous hub that pools resources toward a single institution or organization to focus DOD support and leverage administrative capabilities, resource coordination for student and faculty opportunities at DOD labs, technology transfer, and engagement with funding programs could be an effective mechanism for increasing engagement of MSIs in DOD R&D.

Findings:
- The DOD and other federal agencies have implemented a diverse suite of interventions that addresses the complexity of capacity needs of MSIs.
- To compete for funding, MSI research capacity needs to encompass research capabilities and instrumentation, maintenance, and administration.

- Programs that target underinvested MSIs should be explicit, set eligibility metrics that identify a maximum of previous support, and set funding levels across tiers or tracks that allow for flexibility and sustainable investments in the institution's research capacity development.
- Consortia across and within MSIs and other institutions leverage institutional capabilities and build infrastructure through collaborative activities and are particularly valuable for capacity building when led by investigators at MSIs.
- The defense R&D workforce can be expanded and strengthened through synergistic programs that create continuous funding sources for trainees (undergraduate, graduate, postdoctoral) and faculty researchers, with a specific target for MSIs. As an example, NIH allots funding for individual trainees or faculty that provides flexibility and independence and covers periods for stability at the trainee level (~3 years) and for the establishment (5+ years) of a research lab. Programs that are decoupled across career levels and previous engagement with an agency's funding can support early, mid-, established, and new researchers.

RECOMMENDATION 4-4: The DOD Under Secretary of Defense for Research and Engineering should create programs for evaluating and assessing MSI institutional capacity building. Specifically, this would include a program that supports the development of a "lessons learned" report on building, operating, and maintaining lab infrastructure to conduct unclassified R&D at MSIs. Special considerations should also be given to the unique ability of many MSIs, such as TCUs, to conduct classified research and to the strategic advantage of geographic locations like institutions that are remote. These additional funds should be aimed at understanding and communicating information relevant to long-term capacity building at MSIs. Information that could be examined in such a report might include best practices for the following:
- **Standardizing and accelerating institutional R&D capability with a focus on physical plant and equipment investments;**
- **Increasing the institutional success rate;**
- **Identifying strategies for developing partnerships with non-R1 MSIs; and**
- **Identifying approaches by institution type (HBCU, TCU, non-R1 MSI), highest degree offered, level of research engagement, and geography.**

REFERENCES

DOD (U.S. Department of Defense). 2023. DOD Budget Request: Defense Budget Materials - FY2023. Under Secretary of Defense (Comptroller). https://comptroller. defense.gov/Budget-Materials/Budget2023/.

DOD. 2024a. DOD Budget Request: Defense Budget Materials - FY2024. Under Secretary of Defense (Comptroller). https://comptroller.defense.gov/Budget-Materials/ Budget2024/.

DOD. 2024b. Federally Funded Research and Development Centers (FFRDC) and University Affiliated Research Centers (UARC). https://rt.cto.mil/ffrdc-uarc/.

James, S.M., and S.R. Singer. 2016. From the NSF: The National Science Foundation's investments in broadening participation in science, technology, engineering, and mathematics education through research and capacity building. *CBE Life Sciences Education*, *15*(3), fe7. https://doi.org/10.1187/cbe.16-01-0059.

NASA (National Aeronautics and Space Administration). 2024. Science Mission Directorate (SMD) Bridge Program. https://science.nasa.gov/researchers/smd-bridge-program/.

NASEM (National Academies of Sciences, Engineering, and Medicine). 2019. *Minority serving institutions: America's underutilized resource for strengthening the STEM workforce.* Washington, DC: The National Academies Press. https://doi.org/10.17226/25257.

NASEM. 2020. *Evaluation of the Minerva Research Initiative.* Washington, DC: The National Academies Press. https://doi.org/10.17226/25482.

NASEM. 2022. *Defense research capacity at historically black colleges and universities and other minority institutions: Transitioning from good intentions to measurable outcomes.* Washington, DC: The National Academies Press. https://doi.org/10.17226/26399.

NASEM. 2024. *Building defense research capacity at historically black colleges and universities, tribal colleges and universities, and minority-serving institutions: Proceedings of three town halls.* Washington, DC: The National Academies Press. https://doi. org/10.17226/27511.

NIH (National Institutes of Health). 2024a. Maximizing Investigators' Research Award (MIRA) (R35). National Institute of General Medical Sciences. https://www.nigms. nih.gov/Research/mechanisms/MIRA/Pages/default.aspx.

NIH. 2024b. Maximizing Opportunities for Scientific and Academic Independent Careers (MOSAIC) (K99/R00 and UE5). National Institute of General Medical Sciences. https://nigms.nih.gov/training/careerdev/Pages/MOSAIC.aspx.

NSF (National Science Foundation). 2011. Perspective on broader impacts. NSF 15-008. https://nsf-gov-resources.nsf.gov/2022-09/Broader_Impacts_0.pdf.

NSF. 2024. NSF Graduate Research Fellowship Program (GRFP). https://www.nsfgrfp.org/.

Tretkoff, E. 2007. NSF's "broader impacts" criterion gets mixed reviews. *American Physical Society News*, *16*(6). https://www.aps.org/publications/apsnews/200706/nsf.cfm.

U.S. Congress. 2021. H.R. 3593 - Department of Energy Science for the Future Act. https:// www.congress.gov/bill/117th-congress/house-bill/3593/.

U.S. Congress. 2022a, June 30. H.R. 7900 (RH) - National Defense Authorization Act for Fiscal Year 2023. Washington, DC: U.S. Government Publishing Office. https://www. govinfo.gov/app/details/BILLS-117hr7900rh.

U.S. Congress. 2022b. H.R. 4346 - Chips and Science Act. https://www.congress.gov/ bill/117th-congress/house-bill/4346.

U.S. Department of Energy. n.d. Reaching a New Energy Sciences Workforce (RENEW). Office of Science. https://science.osti.gov/Initiatives/RENEW.

U.S. Department of Energy. 2023. Funding for Accelerated, Inclusive Research (FAIR). Office of Science. https://science.osti.gov/Initiatives/FAIR.

5

Setting a Path Forward for Assessment and Decision-Making

Systemic issues persist that impact of the ability of the Department of Defense (DOD), minority-serving institutions (MSIs), and their respective communities to assess existing capabilities, make decisions, and support growth in capacity for defense-related research and development (R&D). Previous reports have spotlighted challenges with collecting and utilizing data and operationalizing frameworks that effectively assess and articulate existing capabilities. Historical inequities in decision-making within the DOD and other federal agencies have further engrained inaccurate perceptions of MSIs that have hindered their growth in the R&D landscape.

This chapter describes several intervention mechanisms that target institutional planning and practices, decision-making at the DOD, more equitable facilities and administration (F&A) recuperation, and effective frameworks for data collection on MSI capabilities.

ADAPTING A RESOURCE-BASED ASSESSMENT OF MSIs

In considering approaches in how to identify the assets that MSIs bring to the DOD, the committee turned to the Resource-Based Theory of Competitive Advantage. This seminal theory in the field of organizational development was first developed by Robert W. Grant more than 30 years ago. It emphasizes the importance of an organization's internal resources and capabilities to achieve a sustainable competitive advantage, and purports the long-term success for an organization is grounded in use of internal resources to contribute to its higher productivity. Moreover, it can account for the differentiations in internal resources (Barney, 1991) that would be expected at varying types of MSIs. The theory is also supported by the literature on the impact of internal resources on organizational success (Holdford, 2018).

Overview of Grant's Resource-Based Theory of Competitive Advantage

The basis of Grant's theory was built on work nearly a decade earlier by Birger Wernerfelt (1984) who posited that organizations could outperform rivals when they leveraged unique, valuable, rare, or difficult-to-imitate resources and capabilities. Historical research in the field began with basic SWOT (Strengths, Weaknesses, Opportunities, Threats) analysis methods. This approach allows organizations to maximize internal strengths and external opportunities while concurrently mitigating threats and avoiding weaknesses (Barney, 1991). Two schools of thought around organizational competitiveness existed prior to Grant's work: a resource-based model and an environmental model (Barney, 1991).

The environmental model has several assumptions that are not applicable or relevant to MSIs and, in many aspects, all institutions of higher education (IHEs). One key assumption in an environmental model is that organizations in a specific field have the same relevant resources and use the same strategies to pursue competitiveness (Barney, 1991). This is not the case with MSIs, where evidence supports systemic occurrences of under-funding or under-resourcing (Adams and Tucker, 2022). Moreover, MSIs have not only unique student bodies but also difficult-to-imitate intellectual resources and human capital given the demographic composition of their institutions.

In contrast, the resource-based model examines the relationships between performance and an organization's internal resources, which allows a differentiation between organizations rather than the perceived homogeneity that an environmental model assumes (Barney, 1991). As such, the Resource-Based Theory of Competitive Advantage has emerged as a counter to the traditionalist research in strategic management because it is more responsive to the individuality that exists across industries, organizations, and the assets that each organization is able to capitalize or maximize for its own benefit. Environmental models for competitive advantage do not consider these differentiating factors or variables.

Understanding the Key Elements of
the Resource-Based Theory in the MSI Context

Five elements of contextual significance in Grant's Resource-Based Theory of Competitive Advantage apply to MSIs.

First, as noted above, understanding the heterogeneity among organizations is foundational; *resource heterogeneity* means organizations possess different types of resources and capabilities that lead to performance variations. The performance effects of an organization's strategy depend on the firm's individual resources and capabilities and setting within which it is operating. For MSIs, this principle undergirds the equity-centered approach taken during the 2022 National Academies' consensus study *Defense Research Capacity at Historically Black Colleges and Universities and Other Minority Institutions* and its resulting recommendations and findings (NASEM, 2022).

The second principle of relevance is *resource immobility*, in which resources and organizational capabilities may be difficult for competitors to obtain or replicate. The social complexities that contribute to the factors and characteristics of MSIs are part of that immobility.

The third principle is the role of a *value, rarity, inimitability, and organization (VRIO) framework*. Through this framework, organizations can assess their resources and capabilities to determine their sustained competitive advantage that could result in increased R&D or cooperative agreement funding acquisition. What is most critical to this assessment framing is that an organization's rare and irreplicable resources must be organized to provide a sustainable advantage, thus implying the need for internal systems.

The fourth principle relevant to MSIs is the *dynamic capabilities* of an organization. Not only do organizations need to possess valuable resources, but they also need the ability to adapt, reconfigure, or renew their resource base in response to changing market conditions or competitive pressures. For MSIs this includes being able to adapt academic programming or offerings, reconfigure infrastructural operations for R&D, and be dynamic enough to respond to changes in emerging or shifting science and engineering fields.

The fifth relevant principle in Grant's Resource-Based Theory of Competitive Advantage is the role of *strategic implications*. This concept emphasizes the need for an organization to focus internally on developing and leveraging its unique strengths rather than chasing external opportunities. The strategic focus on internal strengths is operationalized as investing in human capital, technology, brand, or other intangible assets. For an MSI, this means not only research faculty and staff but also technology for a culture in which human capital can thrive.

More contemporary work in the Resource-Based Theory of Competitive Advantage purports that "successful innovations are determined not just by the innovation [but are] also the result of the people involved, the organization(s) behind the innovation, contextual factors surrounding its implementation and dissemination, and the innovation's benefits to stakeholders and the firm" (Holdford, 2018, p.1351). When applied to higher education, with its several layers of management (federal, state, local boards, etc.), the Resource-Based Theory of Competitive Advantage makes sense for MSIs that are within these systems. The Resource-Based Theory of Competitive Advantage helps to contextualize what the resources of an institution will include. For example, the intellectual capital of an MSI includes its human capital like faculty and staff experience or skills, executive processes and practices, and information repositories (Ahmadi et al., 2012; Lynch, 2015).

All of these were elements captured in the consensus study's work to gauge the needs of MSIs in their engagement with the DOD. According to the Resource-Based Theory of Competitive Advantage, the way an organization leverages its resources, as well as its ability to provide internal resources, will give it a competitive edge over other organizations.

RECOMMENDATION 5-1: MSIs that seek to increase their R&D footprint, elevate across Carnegie Classifications, and/or improve the rate at which they secure funding should develop an internal strategic plan that advances their R&D goals and clearly articulates their unique value. Such plans could include the following elements:

- **Principles of the Resource-Based Theory of Competitive Advantage.**
- **An institutional SWOT analysis or other strategic analysis to identify specific areas of DOD interest in which its capabilities could have outsized impact.**
- **A 10-year roadmap to guide and prioritize internal investments and engagement with relevant DOD sponsors. Investments could include infrastructure, instrumentation, personnel, curriculum, and/or services.**
- **For institutions with demonstrated need, the DOD and other federal agencies should provide grants for institutional assessment and strategic planning toward increased research engagement and capacity building.**

ADDRESSING POTENTIAL BIASES IN
AWARD DECISION-MAKING

Efficient decision-making is an absolute necessity as it impacts an organization's ability to make choices that have the most impactful outcomes. This is particularly true in the context of the DOD. Warfighters engaged in battle must make split-second decisions to survive. A challenge for the DOD is that fast decision-making on the battlefield does not necessarily translate to the slow progression of thinking that happens in the research enterprise.

In new and complex situations, people tend to rely on previous experience in making split-second decisions about what to do (Williams, 2010). Nobel Prize recipient Daniel Kahneman delineated between two types of thinking and decision-making: fast, intuitive, and emotional as compared with slower, more deliberative, and more logical (Kahneman, 2011). Successful warfighters train to develop fast thinking. They are exposed to every imaginable situation to develop heuristics that will be almost reflexive in decision-making speed for battlefield success and survival (Williams, 2010). In contrast, research and discovery requires a deliberate, thoughtful process that evolves over time. Scientists train to be skeptical and slow thinkers. They train to avoid implicit bias by sharing ideas with others and having others replicate and question their methods and assumptions.

Many DOD decision-makers controlling the resources that are deployed to the research enterprise are individuals who came up through the military ranks and were trained and successful in using heuristics to think fast. Several participants shared with the committee their perspectives that heuristics-based fast thinking, while essential in many life-threatening situations, may lead to implicit biases that result in optimal, bad, or prejudicial decisions. Personnel from the Department of Energy and from the National Institutes of Health described training for program managers (PMs) and peer reviewers designed to examine and reduce implicit bias in proposal evaluation. An evaluation of the practices of PMs and decision-makers within the DOD that assesses the strategies used in the planning, development, and execution of R&D programs that support IHEs is necessary to develop interventions that better support increasing the number and types of institutions supported by the DOD.

In the DOD research enterprise, although a formal review process following a request for proposals is often employed, the PM still holds some autonomy to make funding decisions in allocation and de-allocation of resources. It is not simply a model where the low bidder wins the grant or contract, or the best proposal offered wins the grant or contract. PMs use their own heuristics to assess the likely return on investment given the costs, the personnel, and the approach. With this autonomy and under pressure to show a return on investment for the resources they manage, participants shared their perception that PMs may rely on their fast thinking methods in award decisions. An analogy might be a stockbroker who is deciding whether to invest in blue chip stocks (i.e., known performers that are universities with billion-dollar research enterprises in this context) or startups (i.e., universities newer to the research game or that have low research expenditures). As is well documented, resources at U.S. universities are unequally distributed. The top 30 institutions in terms of R&D expenditures represent less than 3 percent of all IHEs yet account for about 42 percent of the total spent on R&D expenditures (NSF, 2023). The autonomy of PMs that allows for heuristics-based decision-making could be one causal factor that, over time, has led to this unequal distribution of resources. It is simply more expedient, and may seem less risky, to invest in the universities that are known performers than to seek out "startups" and universities newer to the research game.

Decision-makers could be incentivized to create diverse funding portfolios that include both the known performers (R1 universities) and the "startups" (non-R1 universities), or this could be a factor in their performance assessments. While these startups may come with greater risk, the opportunity for greater return on investment is also present. As outlined in Chapter 3, MSIs currently possess a diversity of capabilities that, if invested in, will yield dividends for the DOD through workforce development and novel approaches to pressing concerns of national security. Non-R1 MSIs that have yielded a high return include institutions such as North Carolina Agricultural and Technical State University, Morgan State University, and Howard University, the latter of which has been awarded as the lead of the first Historically Black College and University (HBCU)-led University Affiliated Research Center. Having a diverse portfolio of universities in the funding profile will help mitigate risk. As the 2022 National Academies' report recommended (NASEM, 2022), these startups do require long-term investments due to historical underfunding in physical infrastructure and human capital. Hence, when PMs add these startup universities to their portfolio, they need to acknowledge the challenges that can come with the execution of the research at the university, while recognizing the value-add in the expertise and perspective of the institution that is part of the portfolio. The PM must support and give the startup time and opportunity to build a resilient infrastructure, and more resources need to be provided to PMs to allow for greater risk to be taken in support of increasing the type and number of institutions supported. By having a diverse portfolio, natural mentor-mentee relationships can develop between established and startup universities to give PMs an effective yield on their investments.

RECOMMENDATION 5-2: The DOD should intentionally engage MSIs as part of its R&D portfolio to competitively seek the broadest range of ideas and innovators possible. Increasing the diversity of institutions and researchers actively engaged in DOD's research ecosystem will support increased global competition, undergird national security, and increase innovations that protect the warfighter. In implementing this increased engagement, the following factors should be included:

- Metrics on the number of current and new grant awards and contracting programs to IHEs, with coding to identify MSIs by type, on an annual basis beginning in FY2026. Data should also capture dollar amounts for each award to establish a baseline for growth that dates back to FY2011.
- A tangible goal, set annually by the Office of the Under Secretary of Defense for Research and Engineering, for growing the awards and contracts granted to MSIs as the lead applicants for funding opportunities for each program.
- An assessment by the Office of the Under Secretary of Defense for Research and Engineering of MSI success rates and program performer diversity at the end of each fiscal year. This metric can address DOD's needs by capturing MSI engagement and project relevance to the Department's mission as data for goal-setting in subsequent fiscal years.
- The introduction of training on best practices and implicit bias. The incorporation of best practices and training to address implicit bias in the grant-making process will equip PMs with tools to ensure assessments of institutions and funding decisions are devoid of any implicit biases that may impact proposals from previously under engaged institutions.

ADDRESSING INEQUITIES IN F&A RATES

An important aspect of increasing research capacity at any IHE is receiving adequate support to both conduct research and invest in that institution's F&A. Often referred to as "indirect costs," or IDCs, negotiated F&A rates allow institutions to assess their existing research infrastructure and their built and human capital. Set percentages of F&A rates ensure that funds that are being received via mechanisms such as grants include enough reimbursement to support the current infrastructure fully. To ensure that an institution is receiving an adequate level of IDC reimbursement, it must negotiate its F&A rate with the federal government using either a short form or long form calculation. Short form calculations are a simplified method of calculating F&A rates that are typically reserved for institutions that receive less than $10 million in federal funding and use salary and wages to calculate their direct costs. The long form method is a more extensive calculation that requires more time to prepare, includes a space survey, and is more granular in how total direct costs are identified. While requiring more resources, the long form methodology allows for the most accurate accounting of existing research infrastructure and thus ensures that institutions can recover the maximum amount of funding available to maintain and support growth in their F&A.

The Negotiated Indirect Cost Rate Agreement and subsequent rates are generally negotiated between institutions and an agency representative of the federal government. They play a crucial role in sustaining the research enterprise by reimbursing universities for expenses that cannot be directly attributed to specific research projects but are incurred through the facilitation of research or sponsored programs. Significant differences in F&A rates between different types of institutions exist, particularly between research-intensive (R1) universities and HBCUs, Tribal Colleges and Universities (TCUs), and non-R1 Hispanic-Serving Institutions (HSIs). These differences have far-reaching implications for the ability of non-R1 institutions to build administrative and research infrastructure, and ultimately provide equitable educational opportunities for their students that support skill attainment toward capable defense-related research workforce regardless of the institution that students choose to attend.

F&A rates can be traced back to the 1940s, when the federal government first recognized the need to reimburse universities for the IDCs associated with conducting federally sponsored research. The Office of Naval Research negotiated the first set of principles for determining IDC rates in 1947, which became known as the Blue Book. In 1958, the Bureau of the Budget (now the Office of Management and Budget) issued Circular A-21, establishing official guidelines for determining allowable IDCs at colleges and universities (U.S. Federal Register, 2000). In 2014, the Office of Management and Budget introduced the Uniform Guidance (2 CFR Part 200), which consolidated and streamlined the guidelines for federal grants management. The Uniform Guidance includes the cost principles for determining allowable F&A costs, with specific provisions for colleges and universities (U.S. Federal Register, 2014).

In 2019, the Council on Government Relations (COGR), an association of the largest research institutions, published *Excellence in Research: The Funding Model, F&A Reimbursement, and Why the System Works* (COGR, 2019). As the title indicates, COGR supports the F&A model. From input in the open sessions, Request for Information results, and their own experiences, committee members have found this system seems to work best for institutions that have more than $15 million in research expenditures, but it neither works well nor is inclusive for other institutions below that threshold.

Calculating F&A Rates

F&A rates are calculated based on an institution's indirect expenditure infrastructure and support services costs divided by their direct costs. These expenditure costs are grouped into various categories, such as depreciation, utilities, libraries, and administrative expenses. The difference between negotiating an F&A rate based on Modified Total Direct Costs (MTDC) versus salaries, wages, and fringe benefits, or just salaries and wages, lies in the cost base used to calculate and apply the F&A rate.

Modified Total Direct Costs: MTDC is the most commonly used base for calculating and applying F&A rates. It includes all direct salaries and wages, applicable fringe benefits, materials and supplies, services, travel, and up to the first $25,000 of each subaward (regardless of the period of performance of the subawards under the award). MTDC excludes equipment, capital expenditures, charges for patient care, rental costs, tuition remission, scholarships and fellowships, participant support costs, and the portion of each subaward in excess of $25,000 (2 CFR §200.68). When an institution negotiates an F&A rate based on MTDC, the rate is applied to the MTDC base of sponsored projects to determine the amount of F&A reimbursement. Significantly, the MTDC rate is only available to institutions that have over $10 million in research expenditures per year. Thus, this threshold excludes many HBCUs, TCUs, and HSIs that are not R1 institutions.

Salaries, Wages, and Fringe Benefits Base: In some cases, institutions may negotiate an F&A rate based on a cost base that includes only salaries, wages, and fringe benefits. This means that the F&A rate is calculated by dividing the total F&A costs by the total salaries, wages, and fringe benefits of sponsored projects. When applying this rate, the institution multiplies the F&A rate by the salaries, wages, and fringe benefits charged to a sponsored project to determine the F&A reimbursement. This results in a lower F&A calculation than MTDC.

Salaries and Wages Base: Occasionally, institutions negotiate an F&A rate based solely on salaries and wages, excluding fringe benefits. In this case, the F&A rate is calculated by dividing the total F&A costs by the total salaries and wages of sponsored projects. The rate is then applied only to the salaries and wages charged to a sponsored project to determine the F&A reimbursement.

Disparities Between R1 Institutions and non-R1 MSIs

While the F&A rate calculation process is uniform across all institutions, there are significant variations in the rates negotiated by different types of institutions. Research-intensive (R1) institutions often have higher F&A rates compared to HBCUs, TCUs, and HSIs that are not R1s. There are several factors that contribute to this related to facilities and administrative support.

R1 institutions typically have not only more extensive and sophisticated research facilities, which result in higher costs for construction, maintenance, and operation, but also the availability of resources to monitor, catalog, and track the facilities. For example, several studies have been conducted regarding space utilization at colleges and universities across the country. State systems like University System of Georgia and the University of North Carolina system have funded studies to support the space utilization of their member institutions (Cheston, 2012; Janks et al., 2012; University System of Georgia, 2013). These studies improve utilization reporting and decision-making. Institutions external to state systems or without the operational infrastructure to develop utilization reports necessary for research and facilities space calculations do not have these costs reflected in their F&A rates. According to the Survey of Science and Engineering Research Facilities in 2019,[1] colleges and universities reported an average of 314,732ft^2 in research space. Underlying that average, however,

---

[1] 2019 data used for consistency across National Center for Science and Engineering Statistics Survey databases.

R1 institutions averaged 1,193,551ft², while non-R1 MSIs averaged less than one-tenth that amount, or 108,622ft². Those that can capture the extensiveness of their facilities fare better with their rates. Smaller under-re-sourced MSIs such as TCUs often lack the resources to invest in state-of-the-art research infrastructure and the capacity to capture current facilities, leading to lower F&A rates.

R1 institutions also have larger and more complex research adminis-tration operations, with dedicated staff to handle grant management, com-pliance, and other support functions. According to the National Science Foundation (NSF) National Center for Science and Engineering Statistics, the average number of R&D personnel and staff at colleges and universities was 785 in 2019 (NSF, 2021a). However, R1 institutions reported 10 times more R&D personnel and staff than non-R1 MSIs, averaging around 4,587 compared to 421, respectively. These administrative costs are included in the F&A rates. Many HBCUs, TCUs, and non-R1 HSIs have smaller research portfolios, limited resources in personnel capacity, and less administrative support, resulting in lower calculated administrative costs and F&A rates.

Disparities in F&A rates have significant consequences for HBCUs, TCUs, and non-R1 HSIs (Figure 5-1). According to NSF Higher Education Research and Development (HERD) Survey data in 2019, colleges and universities reported recovering an average of $20,044,000 in IDCs (NSF, 2021b). Carnegie R1 institutions recovered an average $100,227,000, and non-R1 MSIs recovered an average $3,495,000. In other words, R1 institutions are recovering 33 times more in IDCs that they can use to reinvest, support equipment purchases or maintenance costs, hire new staff, or build and update facilities. Lower F&A reimbursements mean that MSIs have fewer resources to invest in building and maintaining research infrastructure, hiring administrative staff, and providing support services for researchers. This creates a self-perpetuating cycle in which MSIs struggle to compete for research funding, which in turn limits their ability to grow their research programs and negotiate higher F&A rates.

The differences in F&A rates can exacerbate existing inequities in higher education. TCUs, as an example, which primarily serve Native American students, often have limited financial resources and face unique challenges in providing educational opportunities to their communities. Lower F&A reimbursements further strain these resources, making it difficult for TCUs to offer their students competitive research opportunities and support services. The Tribally Controlled Community Colleges Assistance Act of 1978 (25 U.S.C. 1801) was designed to provide federal funding for the

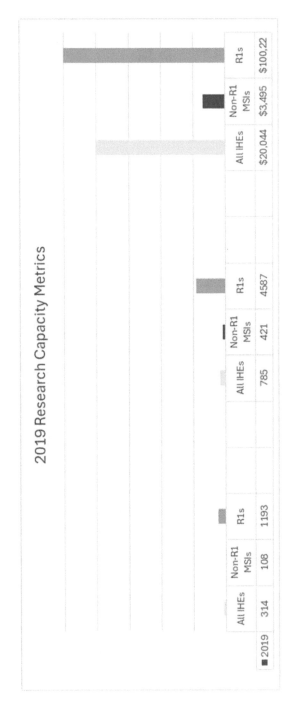

FIGURE 5-1 F&A disparities between R1 and non-R1 MSIs (thousands).
SOURCE: NSF, 2021b.

operation and improvement of TCUs. However, this funding has not kept pace with the growth and evolving needs of TCUs, particularly in research infrastructure and support. As noted in Chapter 2, similar long-standing disparities exist for HBCUs.

Furthermore, federal research funding has traditionally been skewed toward R1 institutions, with MSIs receiving a disproportionately small share of research grants. This is partly due to the competitive nature of research funding, where institutions with established research programs and infrastructure have an advantage in securing grants. The lack of research funding for MSIs has made it challenging for these institutions to build the necessary infrastructure and administrative support to compete effectively for grants.

Findings:
- The F&A system seems to work best for institutions that have more than $15 million in research expenditures, but it neither works well nor is inclusive for other institutions below that threshold.
- An MSI seeking to grow its research enterprise should undergo a renegotiation of its existing F&A rates using long form calculations to calculate its existing infrastructure more accurately for more equitable research administration fund recuperation.
- MSIs should allocate resources to conduct periodic renegotiations to ensure that current F&A rates continue to reflect evolving research infrastructure.

RECOMMENDATION 5-3: To support the growth and development of research programs at MSIs, Congress should provide dedicated funding to help HBCUs, TCUs, and non-R1 HSIs build and maintain state-of-the-art research facilities and equipment. This investment will enable MSIs to compete more effectively for research grants. An example of a program that can be adapted is the 1890 Facilities Grant Program. A similar funding mechanism will provide support for the development and improvement of facilities, equipment, and libraries necessary to conduct defense-related research.
- **Congress should also evaluate the effectiveness of the existing F&A de minimis rate[2] and set a de minimis rate that does the following:**

---

[2] The de minimis IDC rate is 10 percent of an organization's MTDC: 2 CFR 200.414.

- o **Allows for institutions seeking to increase R&D activity to receive a more adequate reimbursement for engagement in federally funded R&D.**
- o **Is higher for smaller institutions to support increased engagement in federally funded R&D.**
- **Additionally, federal agencies should implement an F&A Cost Rate Support Project to provide ongoing technical assistance and support to MSIs in developing and negotiating their F&A rates. The basis of F&A rates for MSIs should be different than for other institutions because institutions with historic investments by states and the federal government benefit from the current structure while MSIs continue to suffer current inequities that are a direct consequence of prior investment disparities in research-focused facilities, equipment, and infrastructure. This will help ensure these historically disadvantaged institutions receive more appropriate F&A reimbursements for their research activities and increase their ability to contribute to U.S. R&D, global competition, and national security.**

INCREASING DATA COLLECTION ON MSI CAPABILITIES

The National Academies' study *Defense Research Capacity at Historically Black Colleges and Universities and Other Minority Institutions* (NASEM, 2022) discussed the need for more data to adequately assess and monitor ongoing efforts to build research capacity and increase the DOD research dollars going to HBCUs, TCUs, and HSIs. The report served as a cornerstone for the current study; it not only underscored the need for more data but also served as a compass to establish a baseline with data and metrics. With the right data and performance indicators, progress toward goals can be more effectively evaluated. Thus, the committee aimed to address a principle conclusion from the 2022 report: "There is insufficient data collection, inter-departmental program coordination, long-term records, and a lack of quantitative evaluations to appropriately assess the DOD's (Under Secretary of Defense for Research and Engineering, military departments, and defense agencies) total investment and measurable impact on the advancement of HBCU/MI research capacity" (NASEM, 2022). As the committee embarked on implementing a framework for measurement and evaluation, it leaned heavily on the previous study as the standard for data and, with a few enhancements, the metrics used to assess progress. The

2022 National Academies' report comprehensively documented a number of data sources, acknowledging their limitations and biases. One departure articulated here is to initiate an effort to gather data directly from the DOD. Constructing this new dataset can help directly confront the biases and limitations identified in current DOD data sources. This represents a significant step forward in the ability to measure and evaluate progress in terms of DOD funding for MSIs.

The data flow diagram (Figure 5-2) introduced below is that of an inverted pyramid. The final product is a dashboard combining the backend database with a frontend interface or dashboard. This dashboard, designed with customer needs in mind, allows the user to query and analyze the data. It could be a user-friendly application through which DOD personnel and other interested stakeholders can monitor and measure the progress by the DOD toward decreasing the R&D gap in dollar amounts awarded to majority institutions (i.e., R1s and others that have the highest DOD research expenditures) compared with MSIs. This tool can empower DOD policymakers to make informed decisions and drive positive change in the research funding landscape. When quantifying the gaps, the strategies for building capacity may emerge that help reduce the R&D gap—for example, new programs with graduate students or more research space and equipment. The caretaker for the data and tool should be a DOD-specific entity. A potential organization is the Defense Manpower Data Center where the data could be collected, updated, and stored. Moreover, the dashboard should be maintained and available for policymakers and their staff to access and analyze the information.

The 2022 National Academies' study also included a recommendation to increase and measure the capacity of HBCUs, HSIs, TCUs, and other MSIs to address the engineering, research, and development needs of the DOD (NASEM, 2022, Recommendation 3C). The report stated that data collection and analyses should be performed on a continual basis for all DOD grants and contracts across all IHEs and should result in a formal annual report to the Office of the Secretary of Defense and Congress early in the calendar year to inform the development of future National Defense Authorization Acts and appropriation bills.

The current committee developed a four-part roadmap to guide the creation of a data-driven dashboard for the DOD that would inform its progress in closing the gap in R&D dollars awarded to MSIs (Figure 5-2).

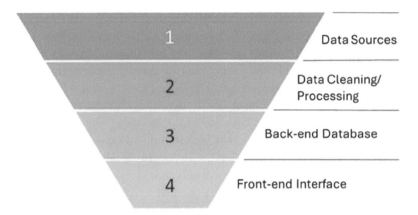

FIGURE 5-2 Four-part roadmap to create a data-driven dashboard.
SOURCE: Committee-generated.

The data-related processes outlined in 1 and 2 in the framework above include

- gathering the data,
- updating information, and
- adding additional information to the dataset as appropriate.

The DOD should link the back-end database (3) and the front-end interface (4) in order to retrieve and analyze the data.

The result of these activities is a tool used by DOD decision-makers to monitor and measure the degree to which the DOD mandate to promote defense research at HBCUs, TCUs, HSIs, and other MSIs is accomplished using the datasets produced.

Data Sources

The committee identified 11 sources of data (Table 5-1). The first seven were described in the 2022 report, and the final four were created from additional NSF and DOD sources. Furthermore, new information could be collected and added to the dataset, such as the number of proposals submitted and the number of awards received.

TABLE 5-1 Sources of Data Related to MSI R&D Expenditures

#	SOURCE	DESCRIPTION OF DATA
1	USAspending.gov	Data on contracts and grants for institutions of higher education (IHEs)
2	National Science Foundation (NSF)	Information related to institutional capacity and to compare federal funding for different types of institutions
3	Integrated Postsecondary Education Data System (IPEDS)	Used to consolidate recipient organization names and link the transaction dataset to other supplementary datasets
4	D&B Hoovers	Additional resource to assist with consolidating recipient organization names
5	Committee's Minority Institution Identifier	Served as the primary identifier of the IHE category for the study
6	Rutgers Center for Minority Serving Institutions Directory of Institutions	Categorizes IHEs that were not already labeled as either MSIs or HBCUs using the committee-provided list
7	Carnegie Classification	Obtained to further delineate differences between institutions on the basis of the type of degrees awarded as well as the character of the research and scholarly activity
8	Multidisciplinary University Research Initiative (MURI)	Data on the number of proposals submitted and the number of awards received
9	Defense University Research Instrumentation Program (DURIP)	Data on the number of proposals submitted and the number of awards received
10	HBCU-MSI	Data on the number of proposals submitted and the number of awards received
11	NSF Higher Education Research and Development (HERD)	Data on the number of proposals submitted and the number of awards received

SOURCE: Committee-generated.

Data Cleaning/Processing

At the Data Cleaning and Processing stage, the DOD can develop four datasets that can be used to create the back-end database in Step 3 (see Figure 5-2). These datasets include the following:

1.   Transactional dataset from USAspending.gov in conjunction with the appended supplementary datasets
2.   NSF HERD (stand-alone)
3.   MURI/DURIP/HBCU-MSI winners dataset
4.   NSF Major Research Instrumentation (MRI) dataset

Back-end Database

Data tables would be created from the four datasets (Figure 5-3). The data tables are used in a back-end relational database to allow querying of the datasets. Building the back-end database to store, manage, and retrieve the data used involves ensuring that the datasets have common data that can be used to create the relationships in the database and that naming conventions are standard across all data tables.

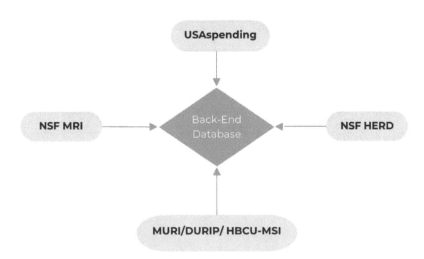

FIGURE 5-3 Back-end database.
SOURCE: Committee-generated.

Front-end Interface

A front-end interface that the user will directly interact with would include the following items to allow the user to query the back-end database (Figure 5-4):

- A web-based user dashboard
- A query processing module
- An application programming interface (API)

In the dashboard, an input link or form accesses the data and allows the user to download and examine the requested data. As an initial check on the accuracy of the data, the data returned to the user will replicate the data used in the 2022 report. The API allows the user to create queries from the back-end database that will produce the required output in the form of spreadsheets, reports, or structured data that can be analyzed in a data analysis system.

Final Product

The final product structurally connects the front-end interface (4) to the back-end database (3) to allow a researcher to create the required queries to provide a more accurate assessment of ongoing efforts to build research capacity and increase the DOD research dollars going to HBCUs, HSIs, TCUs, and other MSIs. Outputs can include datasets based on queries or

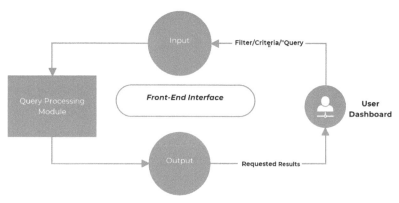

FIGURE 5-4 Front-end interface.
SOURCE: Committee-generated.

visual graphics such as a heat map to help decision-makers easily visualize outcomes.

CONCLUDING THOUGHTS

The committee considered both qualitative and quantitative approaches in closing disparities in research funding and more effectively engaging a diverse range of MSIs in the DOD ecosystem. The Grant Resource-Based Theory of Competitive Advantage suggests a pathway to consider and build upon the unique capabilities of each institution. If DOD PMs are incentivized to build a portfolio of funded efforts, rather than heuristically preferring the larger "known quantities," the institutions that may be more high-risk, high-reward could become more involved in DOD R&D, to the benefit of all.

Additionally, F&A reimbursement should be set up so as not to create a self-perpetuating cycle in which MSIs struggle to compete for research funding. This limits an MSI's ability to grow its research programs and negotiate higher F&A rates. Finally, because data collection and analysis is important to set goals and measure progress, a four-step process is suggested for further development.

REFERENCES

Adams, S., and H. Tucker. 2022, February 1. How America cheated its Black colleges. *Forbes.* https://www.forbes.com/sites/susanadams/2022/02/01/for-hbcus-cheated-out-of-billions-bomb-threats-are-latest-indignity/?sh=67df020b640c.

Ahmadi, F., B. Parivizi, and B. Meyhami. 2012. Intellectual capital accounting and its role in creating competitive advantage at the universities. *VIRTUAL*, *1*(1), 894-912. https://sid.ir/paper/660506/en.

Barney, J. 1991. Firm resources and sustained competitive advantage. *Journal of Management*, *17*(1), 99-120.

Cheston, D. 2012. Students in space: Universities build a lot of classrooms, but use them infrequently. The John William Pope Center for Higher Education Policy. http://www.popecenter.org/commentaries/article.html?id=2757.

COGR (Council on Governmental Relations). 2019. Excellence in research: The funding model, F&A reimbursement, and why the system works. https://www.cogr.edu/sites/default/files/ExcellenceInResearch4_12_19_0.pdf.

Holdford, D.A. 2018. Resource-based theory of competitive advantage—a framework for pharmacy practice innovation research. *Pharmacy Practice* (Granada), *16*(3).

Janks, G., M. Lockhart, and A.S. Travis. 2012. New metrics for the new normal: Rethinking space utilization within the University System of Georgia. http://search.proquest.com.proxygw.wrlc.org/docview/1519532559/C22AF8746AB48DBPQ/5?accountid=112.

Kahneman, D. 2011. Thinking, fast and slow. New York: Farrar, Straus and Giroux.

Lynch, E. 2015. Innovation management: Implications for management practices for the servant leader in education. *Journal of Interdisciplinary Education, 14*(1), 40-71.

NASEM (National Academies of Sciences, Engineering, and Medicine). 2022. *Defense research capacity at historically black colleges and universities and other minority institutions: Transitioning from good intentions to measurable outcomes.* Washington, DC: The National Academies Press. https://doi.org/10.17226/26399.

NSF (National Science Foundation). 2021a. Higher education research and development: Fiscal year 2019. NSF 21-314. National Center for Science and Engineering Statistics. https://ncses.nsf.gov/pubs/nsf21314.

NSF. 2021b. Higher education research and development (HERD) survey 2021. National Center for Science and Engineering Statistics. https://ncses.nsf.gov/surveys/higher-education-research-development/2021.

NSF. 2023. R&D expenditures at U.S. universities increased by $8 billion in FY 2022. National Center for Science and Engineering Statistics. https://ncses.nsf.gov/pubs/nsf24307.

University System of Georgia. 2013, July. The University System of Georgia space utilization initiative. http://www.usg.edu/facilities/documents/USG_SpaceUtilizationInitiative_July2013.pdf.

U.S. Federal Register. 2000. Circular A-21: Cost Principles for Educational Institutions. Office of Management and Budget.

U.S. Federal Register. 2014. Title 2: Grants and Agreements. Code of Federal Regulations. 2 CFR Part 200.

Wernerfelt, B. 1984. A resource-based view of the firm. *Strategic Management Journal, 5*(2), 171-180.

Williams, B. 2010. Heuristics and biases in military decision making. *Military Review*, September-October, 40-52.

6

Conclusion

As mandated in Section 220 of the FY 2022 National Defense Authorization Act and Section 233 of the FY 2023 National Defense Authorization Act, this study aims to outline specific interventions that can be taken by the Department of Defense (DOD), Historically Black Colleges and Universities (HBCUs), Tribal Colleges and Universities (TCUs), enrollment-defined Minority-Serving Institutions (MSIs), and Congress to increase the participation of MSIs in defense-related research and development (R&D). Where possible, this study will also operationalize targeted strategies that provide the resources for elevation on the Carnegie Classification of Institutions of Higher Education spectrum. Carnegie designations as R1 (very high research activity) and R2 (high research) institutions are solely obtainable for institutions with a diversity of research-focused doctoral programs and that surpass specified thresholds for R&D expenditures. This posed an immediate conundrum in the committee's deliberations, given that a significant portion of MSIs lack doctoral programs or graduate programs altogether. Furthermore, given additional factors such as state legislation, some institutions are unable to increase their doctoral program offerings and are legally unable to obtain R1 status as a result (California State Legislature, 2023). Nevertheless, there are unique opportunities for interventions that can increase the engagement and activity of MSIs in defense-related research.

Recognizing that high-impact academic research is not only centered at R1 and R2 institutions, in 2025, the Carnegie Classification of Institutions of Higher Education will utilize a more comprehensive methodology that introduces a new category entitled "Research Colleges and Universities," allowing for research-engaged institutions to be accurately reflected in the U.S. research enterprise as important contributors to R&D (Carnegie Classifications of Institutions of Higher Education, 2024). Therefore, to address the core intent of the legislation and DOD's activities, the committee centered on opportunities for increasing engagement of the majority of MSIs to support defense-related R&D and national security needs.

Throughout the study process, perspectives from across the DOD, other federal agencies, MSIs, and institutions and industries that receive significant DOD support provided a comprehensive review of the barriers faced by MSIs as they increase their research activities, defense-related or otherwise. They point to how DOD's R&D programs interact with MSIs and what opportunities are currently available so that MSIs can contribute to DOD's existing R&D infrastructure.

The committee found that there are indeed significant barriers to MSI engagement in federal R&D, but there are also opportunities to provide unique engagement mechanisms that leverage their strengths in research and personnel (faculty, students) and support sustainable capacity development. For example, the legislation and committee's statement of task initially called for the committee to address "DOD's engineering and research and development needs" and increase "defense-related research activities" at MSIs. However, defense-related research activities not only are more comprehensive by discipline but also extend outside of the DOD to science funding agencies that support basic and applied research that contributes to the Department's mission and Critical Technology Areas (CTAs). Moreover, to ensure sustainability in defense-related research capacity development at MSIs, successful interventions should leverage activities across the federal government and identify ways that investments in MSI capabilities for basic and applied research outside of the DOD can be used to make institutions more prepared to support DOD's needs.

The 2022 National Academies of Sciences, Engineering, and Medicine report *Defense Research Capacity at Historically Black Colleges and Universities and Other Minority Institutions: Transitioning from Good Intentions to Measurable Outcomes* outlined several important factors necessary for increasing research capacity at MSIs. In addition to defining the components of research activity across previous Carnegie Classifications, the report identified a framework for effective ancillary services that allow an institution to facilitate federal grants. The report highlighted the need for long-term support to counteract a history of underinvestment, increase real funding for basic research and HBCU/ Minority Institution (MI)-centered programs, and develop better data tracking mechanisms to evaluate existing HBCU/MI programs administered by the Department.

Additional reports have identified important internal mechanisms at MSIs, such as sustaining strong, forward-looking leadership with comprehensive strategic planning that aligns resource allocations with national science, technology, engineering, and mathematics (STEM) needs; addressing faculty recruitment and retention through competitive compensation packages; supporting faculty development through research-engaged sabbaticals; and formalizing mentoring to support success. External mechanisms also play an important role in developing and sustaining research infrastructure at MSIs that have been historically underfunded and underutilized. Local, state, and federal agencies involved in research funding and capacity building should provide stable funding for MSI R&D to support local industries and national priorities. Studies have underscored the important role of federal agencies that support academic research and STEM education in developing programs that target MSIs, increase data collection on the effectiveness of said programs, and coordinate through an interagency task force to better leverage efforts across the federal government. Furthermore, to cement sustainability, efforts to develop research capacity at MSIs through federal agencies require a multisectoral approach that includes an equitable coordination across MSIs, federal agencies and labs, and STEM industries.

ADAPTING NON-DOD AGENCY MODELS

The 2022 National Academies' report included recommendations for the Under Secretary of Defense for Research and Engineering to incorporate models used at other science funding agencies (NASEM, 2022). The committee explored several mechanisms through open session discussions and a review of a Town Hall series held in 2023 to identify potential frameworks that could be incorporated into new and existing MSI-focused funding mechanisms. Promising practices included introducing synergistic programs that create continuous funding sources for trainees (undergraduate, graduate, postdoctoral) and faculty researchers, with a specific target for MSIs. Successful funding mechanisms administered by other agencies include support for individual trainees and faculty to provide flexibility and independence with funding periods that provide stability and establish a research lab led by a grantee that can support an agency's mission. Given the diversity of MSIs, with HBCUs, TCUs, Hispanic-Serving Institutions (HSIs), and others exhibiting diversity in barriers and strengths within and across institutional classifications, agencies have implemented a diverse suite of interventions that addresses the complexity of the capacity needs of different MSIs. These targeted programs incorporate the communities' perspectives in planning, developing, administering, and evaluating new and existing capacity development programs. Additionally, agencies that have shown positive growth in their underinvested institution performer base include language in their funding announcements that is explicit and sets eligibility metrics. These eligibility metrics identify a maximum of previous support and set funding levels across tiers or tracks that allow for flexibility and sustainable investments in the institution's research capacity development.

RECOMMENDATIONS

Several barriers have been elucidated in this and prior studies that impact the ability of MSIs to engage meaningfully in federal R&D. These barriers often reflect the lack of resources necessary to adequately support research-engaged faculty and trainees and facilitate ways to increase coordination of the existing research capabilities of MSIs. The committee explored these barriers and developed recommendations that the DOD and MSIs can implement to support the growth of research-engaged faculty and trainees and ensure that MSIs maintain existing missions.

RECOMMENDATION 2-1: The systemic underinvestment in R&D capacity at MSIs, particularly in their infrastructure at the state and federal levels, is a pressing issue. To capture the full potential of MSIs, it is imperative that the DOD, with congressional support, introduce mechanisms for dedicated funding for non-R1 MSIs to foster research infrastructure growth including funding facilities and equipment. Potential forms of support could include the following:

- **Providing direct support for investment in facilities and equipment to increase R&D relevant to national needs for MSIs such as TCUs, which span multiple states, and private HBCUs, which receive less state support than their public counterparts.**
- **Providing matching funds for states to invest in research infrastructure growth at MSIs seeking to increase their research infrastructure. These matching funds will incentivize state and local governments that have fallen short of authorizations, which has led to systemic and inequitable underinvestment in MSIs.**

RECOMMENDATION 3-1: For MSIs to contribute more fully to defense-related research, research capacity and talent must be developed and strengthened. This is a unique strategic opportunity for the DOD and national security. Many MSIs (in particular TCUs) embody distinctive perspectives and so have the potential to make completely unique research contributions in areas such as addressing agricultural systems that are resilient in drought conditions. These distinctive ways of thinking, problem-solving, and social organization should be of interest to both the DOD and the broader scientific community. Investing in investigators at non-R1 MSIs will not only increase the defense-related research capacity base nationally, but also deepen and diversify the available investigators that can support and advance the Department's R&D needs.

- To partially engage this opportunity, the DOD, with support from Congress, should develop and administer a DOD MSI Investigator Award for very capable scholars at HBCUs, TCUs, and MSIs. This new program should be modeled after existing department programs such as the DARPA Young Faculty Award, Air Force Young Investigator Program, and ONR Young Investigator Program. In the implementation of DOD MSI Investigator awards, the following factors should be included:
- Up to 100 awards made per year across the Department's branches (Air Force, Navy, Army, etc.).
- Tracking of the number of awards made to each institution type to guide evaluation, outreach, and programmatic planning.
- An average of $150,000 per grant per year over a 5-year grant period with the option to renew. This sustained funding will include funding that enables each DOD MSI Investigator to establish a research lab at their institution, pursue topics relevant to the DOD's R&D needs, and serve as a focal point for increased engagement for defense-related research.
- Cohorts of investigators should be convened in-person on an annual basis to discuss successes, roadblocks, and recommendations to refine and reshape this program based on the unique and not-well-understood challenges and opportunities at their sites with the identification appropriate metrics for evaluation.
- The focus should be on faculty at HBCUs, TCUs, and non-R1 MSIs with award recipients providing 51 percent of their effort to the funded research project during the duration of the award.

The National Institutes of Health PIONEER award and Howard Hughes Medical Institute Program may serve as models for an agency-wide program that supports promising scientists across career stages in addressing high-risk/high-reward issues relevant to the DOD's mission.

- The DOD should avoid the use of 'tenure track" designated faculty as a criterion. The use of "tenure track" appointments creates a barrier for engagement for smaller institutions such as TCUs. As a result, any program focused on developing researchers at non-R1 MSIs that use "tenure track" as an eligibility criterion would preclude both their engagement from these institutions and the DOD from broadening its potential researcher base.
- Review criteria and processes should be developed with an advisory council that includes researchers and research administrators from MSIs and institutions with historical engagement with the DOD.

RECOMMENDATION 3-2: To support the existing missions of MSIs to educate and provide support for investigator release time, the DOD should develop a postdoctoral fellowship program for MSIs geared toward doctoral recipients with specialized expertise in defense-related research areas, broad disciplinary understanding, and interest in developing instructional skills. Funding that provides relief for course and research support at MSIs will help incentivize institutions where teaching loads prohibit significant engagement in research. It can also help support the careers of postdocs pursuing experience as faculty. The DOD should incorporate the following into the program:

- Recipients can allot 50 percent of their time as a research associate within the lab of a faculty member conducting defense-related research and 50 percent of their time to teach courses typically covered by the investigator.
- The duration of the fellowship should correspond with the length of a typical research grant to ensure continuity in course coverage. It should be affixed to non-R1 primary teaching institutions and DOD-relevant MSI funding mechanisms.
- A matching mechanism that connects prospective fellows with MSI faculty should facilitate awarded fellows' identification of a supervising investigator.

- A postdoctoral mentoring plan should be included. Mentoring plans should be standardized to ensure continuity in support for fellows, and mentors should receive training on mentorship.

RECOMMENDATION 3-3: Inter-institutional collaborations among MSIs are an underutilized strategy to leverage unique perspectives, skills, and abilities to further the DOD research objectives. Frequently, no single institution possesses the necessary breadth of talent to broadly serve the DOD's research needs. Furthermore, under-resourced administrative staff often disincentivize MSI collaborations, especially when a well-resourced Primarily White Institutions R1 is poised to take the lead. To increase capacity development and engagement, the DOD should develop a funding program to support the creation of research consortia with an HBCU, TCU, HSI or other non-R1 MSI lead. The research consortia would focus on a clear area or project and include scholars from three or more MSIs. The committee is aware of the Research Institute for Tactical Autonomy, led by Howard University, an HBCU, and recommends that additional consortia be developed to address research projects of critical need to the DOD to facilitate the engagement of more MSIs. In the implementation of this funding program, the following factors should be included:
- Support for developing consortia that fund R&D.
- Funding for at least 5 years for each consortium to support planning, execution, and evaluation activities.
- Support for consortia that exhibit intentional and equitable collaboration and mutually beneficial partnerships through strategies, including at least 6 months of pre-award communication, partnership agreements, and/or articulated resource and personnel sharing frameworks.
- Planning grants for prospective consortia to develop full proposals.
- Supplements for institutional mentorship between MSIs and known performers to assist with the consortia's planning and implementation.

RECOMMENDATION 3-4: An under-resourced administrative infrastructure to secure, manage, and coordinate grants, contracts, and other opportunities is a significant barrier to engagement in the DOD and other federal agency opportunities. To increase the ability of under-resourced MSIs to adequately and effectively participate in opportunities, the DOD, with congressional support, should develop a funding program to develop administrative hubs. The administrative hubs would allow MSIs the option to coordinate through a professional organization that possesses the administrative expertise and resources necessary to support grant and contract acquisition and management (pre- and post-award). The hubs could also coordinate faculty and student participation in DOD opportunities, and communicate the current and evolving capabilities of member institutions. Additionally, these hubs would be used by three or more non-R1 MSIs that are regionally located or geographically close to facilitate coordination and mutual use and complications due to differences in administrative policies, complexities and protocols need to be built into use agreements. In the implementation of this program, the following factors should be included:

- **Funding for at least 5 years to launch each hub and facilitate planning, execution, and evaluation.**
- **Support for lead organizations with clearly articulated missions relevant to MSIs who exhibit intentional development through strategies, such as the following:**
  - **Referencing at least 6 months of pre-award communication,**
  - **Partnership agreements with participating institutions,**
  - **An administrative capability track record, and**
  - **Clearly defined sustainability plans that demonstrate maintenance and long-term administrative support for participating institutions post-award.**
- **Planning grants for prospective hubs to develop full proposals.**

The DOD has created a tapestry of R&D infrastructure across the nation that advances innovation in research areas of national security. Its labs, University Affiliated Research Centers (UARCs), and Federally Funded Research and Development Centers (FFRDCs) have the potential to provide the infrastructure necessary for sustainable engagement in the Department's research ecosystem.

During the open sessions, the committee found that several DOD programs currently engage with MSIs through outreach activities (e.g., workshops, site visits, conferences). However, this engagement is disparate. To better coordinate this engagement DOD-wide and track and increase success toward more engagement, the committee proposes several strategies for evaluation and coordination that provide interagency coordination and sharing of best practices.

A significant impediment to MSI engagement with DOD R&D is a lack of awareness of the diversity of R&D supported by the Department. When exploring the DOD's CTAs and dissecting the components of each CTA, the committee found that most MSIs possess academic programs equivalent to one or more of these areas. To better engage with DOD R&D, the Department, Congress, and MSIs must conduct a thorough evaluation that matches current programs at MSIs to the basic and applied components of the CTAs. Exploring these areas through internal and external engagement pathways could leverage existing infrastructure, increase the efficacy of outreach activities, and identify a more comprehensive view of R&D that is inclusive across disciplines to increase engagement and advance the DOD's research and workforce needs.

RECOMMENDATION 4-1: Engaging the breadth of research disciplines relevant to national security is necessary to fully explore opportunities and increase MSIs' engagement in defense-related R&D. Congress should create programs that increase the utilization of the full breadth of the DOD's research in non-engineering disciplines.

- **The DOD should further develop its research capacity by including and expanding funding to support the social sciences in its calls for proposals, focusing on the unique perspective MSIs bring to these fields. HBCUs, TCUs, and MSIs can provide rich contributions in the social sciences and other non-engineering-focused disciplines that are critical to DOD research.**

RECOMMENDATION 4-2: Beginning in FY2026, the DOD Under Secretary of Defense for Research and Engineering should collect and publish data annually that measure the efficacy of existing outreach programs targeting MSIs, and share lessons learned with DOD agencies to accelerate the dissemination of best practices.

- **This report should include a longitudinal analysis to provide evidence of successful engagement and impact. Potential metrics should include the following:**
  - **Number of MSIs engaged quarterly,**
  - **Data on personnel interacted with (investigators, administrators, students),**
  - **Institution type,**
  - **Hours and type of engagement,**

o Number of applications received and time to successful award, and
o Measurement of research infrastructure growth among awardees (instrumentation, research-engaged faculty, administration support, etc.).

- Metrics collected should be used to set a baseline for improvement of how the DOD engages with MSIs. They should be assessed annually to direct resources and engagement activities toward increased participation in DOD R&D.
- The DOD Under Secretary of Defense for Research and Engineering should administer new outreach programs that do the following:
  o Create and deploy a DOD liaison to HBCUs, TCUs, and MSIs to translate the DOD's interests to the university and university capabilities and interests to the DOD.
  o Place scientists and engineers from local military labs at MSIs to teach STEM courses and provide course load relief for investigators pursuing and conducting defense-related research, as referenced in Chapter 3. A potential framework could be the use of the Intergovernmental Personnel Act Mobility Program.
- The DOD Under Secretary of Defense for Research and Engineering should expand existing outreach programs so that HBCU, TCU, and MSI employees are eligible for sabbaticals to gain R&D experience with DOD acquisition and operations organizations.

These new outreach programs will allow for increased awareness and provide teaching load relief to HBCU, TCU, and MSI faculty conducting DOD R&D. In doing so, however, the DOD's HBCU/MI programs should address institutions' unique contexts and needs rather than group HBCU, TCU, HSI, and other MSI engagements. A one-size-fits-all approach decreases the successful engagement of MSIs, given the diversity of needs, challenges, engagement, and opportunities within and across MSIs. To plan and implement more granular interventions, the DOD should undertake robust comment periods, listening sessions, and dialogue with institutions and their supporting communities to develop engagement frameworks tailored to each MSI type to increase the Department's success in its engagement with MSIs and relationship development activities. This approach is both in the strategic interest of the DOD and helps support global competitiveness, national security, and historic disparities.

RECOMMENDATION 4-3: The DOD should allocate resources to assess the potential for regional connectivity and partnerships between existing DOD labs, UARCs, and FFRDCs, and local or regional HBCUs, TCUs, and MSIs. This assessment should include collecting metrics on existing and potential research collaborations between these entities.

- Based on this assessment described above, the DOD should provide guidance to DOD labs, UARCs, and FFRDCs about how to support and expand collaborative R&D with MSIs within proximity or sharing similar research foci.
- The DOD should develop a pilot funding opportunity that allows MSI investigators to develop research projects with investigators at DOD labs, UARCs, and FFRDCs. Awards should include MSI investigators as lead investigators, co-investigators, or lead contractors.

RECOMMENDATION 4-4: The DOD Under Secretary of Defense for Research and Engineering should create programs for evaluating and assessing MSI institutional capacity building. Specifically, this would include a program that supports the development of a "lessons learned" report on building, operating, and maintaining lab infrastructure to conduct unclassified R&D at MSIs. Special considerations should also be given to the unique ability of many MSIs, such as TCUs, to conduct classified research and to the strategic advantage of geographic locations like institutions that are remote. These additional funds should be aimed at understanding and communicating information relevant to long-term capacity building at MSIs. Information that could be examined in such a report might include best practices for the following:

- Standardizing and accelerating institutional R&D capability with a focus on physical plant and equipment investments;
- Increasing the institutional success rate;
- Identifying strategies for developing partnerships with non-R1 MSIs; and
- Identifying approaches by institution type (HBCU, TCU, non-R1 MSI), highest degree offered, level of research engagement, and geography.

RECOMMENDATION 5-1: MSIs that seek to increase their R&D footprint, elevate across Carnegie Classifications, and/or improve the rate at which they secure funding should develop an internal strategic plan that advances their R&D goals and clearly articulates their unique value. Such plans could include the following elements:

- Principles of the Resource-Based Theory of Competitive Advantage.
- An institutional SWOT (Strengths, Weaknesses, Opportunities, Threats) analysis or other strategic analysis to identify specific areas of the DOD's interest in which its capabilities could have outsized impact.
- A 10-year roadmap to guide and prioritize internal investments and engagement with relevant DOD sponsors. Investments could include infrastructure, instrumentation, personnel, curriculum, and/or services.
- For institutions with demonstrated need, the DOD and other federal agencies should provide grants for institutional assessment and strategic planning toward increased research engagement and capacity building.

RECOMMENDATION 5-2: The DOD should intentionally engage MSIs as part of its R&D portfolio to competitively seek the broadest range of ideas and innovators possible. Increasing the diversity of institutions and researchers actively engaged in the DOD's research ecosystem will support increased global competition, undergird national security, and increase innovations that protect the warfighter. In implementing this increased engagement, the following factors should be included:

- Metrics on the number of current and new grant awards and contracting programs to institutions of higher education, with coding to identify MSIs by type, on an annual basis beginning in FY2026. Data should also capture dollar amounts for each award to establish a baseline for growth that dates back to FY2011.
- A tangible goal, set annually by the Office of the Under Secretary of Defense for Research and Engineering, for growing the awards and contracts granted to MSIs as the lead applicants for funding opportunities for each program.
- An assessment by the Office of the Under Secretary of Defense for Research and Engineering of MSI success rates and program

performer diversity at the end of each fiscal year. This metric can address the DOD's needs by capturing MSI engagement and project relevance to the Department's mission as data for goal-setting in subsequent fiscal years.
• The introduction of training on best practices and implicit bias. The incorporation of best practices and training to address implicit bias in the grant-making process will equip PMs with tools to ensure assessments of institutions and funding decisions are devoid of any implicit biases that may impact proposals from previously under engaged institutions.

RECOMMENDATION 5-3: To support the growth and development of research programs at MSIs, Congress should provide dedicated funding to help HBCUs, TCUs, and non-R1 HSIs build and maintain state-of-the-art research facilities and equipment. This investment will enable MSIs to compete more effectively for research grants. An example of a program that can be adapted is the 1890 Facilities Grant Program. A similar funding mechanism will provide support for the development and improvement of facilities, equipment, and libraries necessary to conduct defense-related research.
• Congress should also evaluate the effectiveness of the existing F&A de minimis rate[1] and set a de minimis rate that does the following:
  o Allows for institutions seeking to increase R&D activity to receive a more adequate reimbursement for engagement in federally funded R&D.
  o Is higher for smaller institutions to support increased engagement in federally funded R&D.
• Additionally, federal agencies should implement an F&A Cost Rate Support Project to provide ongoing technical assistance and support to MSIs in developing and negotiating their F&A rates. The basis of F&A rates for MSIs should be different than for other institutions because institutions with historic investments by states and the federal government benefit from the current structure while MSIs continue to suffer current inequities that are a direct consequence of prior investment disparities in research-focused facilities, equipment, and infrastructure. This

---

[1] The de minimis IDC rate is 10 percent of an organization's MTDC: 2 CFR 200.414.

will help ensure these historically disadvantaged institutions receive more appropriate F&A reimbursements for their research activities and increase their ability to contribute to U.S. R&D, global competition, and national security.

A PLAN FOR INCREASED ENGAGEMENT IN DOD R&D

The study committee's charge was to conduct an assessment of the activities necessary to increase the engagement of MSIs in defense-related research, where possible, elevate these institutions to R1 status, and identify strategies for tracking and increasing the capacity of MSIs to address the R&D needs of the DOD. Many of the recommendations listed above, particularly drawing from Chapters 4 and 5, center on data collection; additionally, Chapter 5 presents a data collection framework to collect, analyze, and present data related to MSI engagement with the DOD. The committee recognizes these efforts take time and resources on the part of the DOD and institutions. However, when collected and used, these data can help the DOD more effectively assess its current and ongoing impact and better plan its future interventions.

To better understand how MSIs can increase their capacity for R&D, it is essential to identify and address the barriers that have historically impacted their engagement. Many MSIs were developed as teaching institutions, providing the only opportunity for members of the communities they serve to receive an education. Those missions have persisted through times of underfunding and historic marginalization. Regardless of the under-investment and historic missions, MSIs have continued to grow the breadth and scope of their academic offerings and research capacity. Furthermore, HBCUs, TCUs, HSIs, and other MSIs provide a diversity of perspectives that can support innovation and advancements and strengthen the nation's competitiveness and national security. However, to facilitate this innovation and engage these institutions fully, Congress, the DOD, and other federal agencies must address existing barriers, explore unique strategies, and develop frameworks that allow MSIs to grow their capabilities and retain their unique role in the research enterprise.

REFERENCES

California State Legislature. 2023. Assembly Bill No. 656: An Act to add Article 4.92 (commencing with Section 66046) to Chapter 2 of Part 40 of Division 5 of Title 3 of, and to repeal Section 66046.3 of the Education Code, relating to public postsecondary education. https://trackbill.com/bill/california-assembly-bill-656-california-state-university-doctoral-programs/2362694/.

Carnegie Classification of Institutions of Higher Education. 2024. 2025 Research designations. https://carnegieclassifications.acenet.edu/carnegie-classification/research-designations/.

NASEM (National Academies of Sciences, Engineering, and Medicine). 2022. *Defense research capacity at historically black colleges and universities and other minority institutions: Transitioning from good intentions to measurable outcomes.* Washington, DC: The National Academies Press. https://doi.org/10.17226/26399.

Appendix A

Public Meeting Agendas

COMMITTEE ON THE DEVELOPMENT OF A PLAN TO PROMOTE DEFENSE RESEARCH AT HISTORICALLY BLACK COLLEGES AND UNIVERSITIES, TRIBAL COLLEGES AND UNIVERSITIES, HISPANIC-SERVING INSTITUTIONS, AND OTHER MINORITY-SERVING INSTITUTIONS

Virtual
June 2, 2023

12:05–12:50   Sponsor Briefing
- Evelyn Kent – Director of the Department of Defense HBCU/MI Program and Outreach OUSD(R&E)
- Patrice Collins, Ph.D. – DEVCOM ARL Educational Outreach Branch Chief

DEVELOPMENT OF A PLAN TO PROMOTE DEFENSE RESEARCH AT HISTORICALLY BLACK COLLEGES AND UNIVERSITIES, TRIBAL COLLEGES AND UNIVERSITIES, AND HISPANIC-SERVING INSTITUTIONS— SITE VISIT

Fayetteville State University
1200 Murchison Road
Fayetteville, NC 28301

September 18-19, 2023

DAY 1 (EST)

9:30–10:00   Welcome and Introductions
              Ganesh C. Bora, Ph.D., Associate Vice Chancellor for
              Research and Innovation, Chief Research Officer
              Andrea Christelle, Ph.D. – Committee Co-Chair
              Erin Lynch, EdD – Committee Co-Chair

10:00–11:00   Meeting and Discussion with UNCFSU Provost
              Monica Terrell Leach, EdD, Provost
              Committee members

11:00–11:20   Break

11:20–2:45   Tour of Facilities and Departments
              Question themes:
              • Describe the barriers that your institution encounters as
                it pursues increased research engagement.
              • Legislative engagement/strategy
              • Describe your current infrastructure and the
                components required to support/grow your
                institution's research capabilities. (Personnel, facilities,
                administration, etc.)
              • Of what work are you most proud? How to engage
                DOD in the strategic advantage of advancing this
                research?
              • Where would you like to engage but lack resources?

11:20–12:30 Department and Laboratories
             Department of Biological and Forensic Sciences
             Department of Chemistry, Physics and Materials Science
             Department of Mathematics and Computer Science
             Advanced Systems Group
             UNCFSU Department Administrators

             Committee members

12:30–12:45 Break

12:45–2:00   Administrative Offices
             • Research enterprise units:
               o Finance
               o Sponsored Programs
               o Academic Affairs, etc.

               UNCFSU Department Administrators
               Committee members

2:00–2:45   Technology Transfer Capacity/Resources

             UNCFSU Department Administrators
             Committee members

DAY 1 OF VISIT ADJOURNS

DAY 2

9:00–10:00   Welcome and Student/Faculty Research Presentations/Posters

             Ganesh C. Bora, Ph.D., Associate Vice Chancellor for
             Research and Innovation, Chief Research Officer
             UNCFSU Faculty/students
             Committee members

10:00–11:30 Faculty/Student/Administrator Panel

UNCFSU Faculty/students
Committee members

11:30–12:00 Committee Debrief

DAY 2 OF VISIT ADJOURNS

DEVELOPMENT OF A PLAN TO PROMOTE DEFENSE RESEARCH AT HISTORICALLY BLACK COLLEGES AND UNIVERSITIES, TRIBAL COLLEGES AND UNIVERSITIES, AND HISPANIC-SERVING INSTITUTIONS— SITE VISIT

Diné College
1 Circle Dr.
Route 12
Tsaile, AZ 86556

October 25-26, 2023

DAY 1 (MST)

11:30–1:00   Lunch and Introduction to Research Team
• Introduction to Na'al Kaah Bee Honít'i' – Research, Innovation & Practice
  ○ Staff roles and functions
  ○ Priorities, goals, and institutional strategic design

Andrea Christelle, Ph.D. – Committee Co-Chair
Diné Administrators

1:00–2:15   Meeting with Vice Presidents and Deans
• Vision for the institution's future
• Discussion on challenges and opportunities

Patrick Blackwater, Dean of Business and Social Sciences
Karla Britton, Dean of Arts and Humanities
Glennita Haskey, Vice President for Student Affairs
Rex Lee Jim, Dean of Diné Studies and Education
Alysa Landry, Provost
Bo Lewis, Vice President of Finance and Administration
James Tutt, Dean of STEM

2:15–2:30   Break

2:30–3:30   Tour of Land Grant Office and Capital Projects Goals
               Leon Jackson, Director of Capital Projects
               Benita Litson, Director of Land Grant Office

DAY 1 ADJOURNS

DAY 2

8:30–9:00   Breakfast and Welcome
               Monty Roessel, President
               Andrea Christelle, Ph.D. – Committee Co-Chair

9:00–10:30   Research Highlights
               • Faculty and Student Research Presentations
               • Discussions on current academic trends
               • Feedback and concerns from faculty

10:30–10:45   Break

10:45–11:30   Legislative Affairs Presentation
               • **Crystal Carr**, Director of Legislative Affairs and Special
                 Projects
               • **Clara Pratte**, Federal Advocate

11:30   Debrief conversations available with Leadership and
               Research Team

DAY 2 ADJOURNS

DEVELOPMENT OF A PLAN TO PROMOTE DEFENSE RESEARCH AT HISTORICALLY BLACK COLLEGES AND UNIVERSITIES, TRIBAL COLLEGES AND UNIVERSITIES, AND HISPANIC-SERVING INSTITUTIONS— COMMITTEE MEETING OPEN SESSION— DOD STRATEGIC ENGAGEMENT SESSION 1

Virtual

November 3, 2023

1:00–1:10   Welcome
Committee Members

1:10–1:45   DOD Program Discussion

Department of Navy's (DoN) Historically Black Colleges and Universities/Minority Institutions (HBCU/MI) program
Anthony C. Smith, Jr. – Director

1:45–2:50   University-Affiliated Research Center Discussion

Geophysical Institute
Robert McCoy, Ph.D. – Director

Johns Hopkins Applied Physics Laboratory
Ralph Semmel, Ph.D. – Director

2:50–3:00   Recap and Adjourn

DEVELOPMENT OF A PLAN TO PROMOTE DEFENSE RESEARCH AT HISTORICALLY BLACK COLLEGES AND UNIVERSITIES, TRIBAL COLLEGES AND UNIVERSITIES, AND HISPANIC-SERVING INSTITUTIONS— COMMITTEE MEETING OPEN SESSION— DOD STRATEGIC ENGAGEMENT SESSION 2

Virtual

November 8, 2023

11:00–11:10   Welcome
Committee Members

11:10–12:20   DOD Program Discussion

Minerva Research Initiative
David Montgomery, Ph.D.

Defense Advanced Research Projects Agency
Jennifer Thabet

Air Force Office of Scientific Research (AFOSR),
Historically Black Colleges and Universities/Minority
Serving Institutions
Edward J. Lee
Rahel R. Rudd

Defense Threat Reduction Agency
Treniece Terry, Ph.D.

12:20–12:50   Federally Funded Research and Development Center

Aerospace Corporation
John P. Galer

12:50–1:00   Recap and Adjourn

DEVELOPMENT OF A PLAN TO PROMOTE DEFENSE
RESEARCH AT HISTORICALLY BLACK COLLEGES AND
UNIVERSITIES, TRIBAL COLLEGES AND UNIVERSITIES,
AND HISPANIC-SERVING INSTITUTIONS—
COMMITTEE MEETING OPEN SESSION—
DOD DATA COLLECTION AND METRICS
GATHERING SESSION #1

Virtual

November 28, 2023

1:00–1:05   Welcome

Committee Members

1:05–1:25   Carnegie Classification Metrics

American Council on Education
Mushtaq Gunja – Executive Director of the Carnegie
Classification Systems & Senior Vice President
Sara Gast – Deputy Executive Director, Carnegie
Classifications

1:25–2:25   Federal Data Collection and Statistics Programs

National Center for Science and Engineering Statistics –
National Science Foundation
John M. Finamore, Ph.D. – Chief Statistician

National Center for Education Statistics – Department of
Education
Josue De La Rosa – Director, Annual Reports and
Information Staff
Tara Lawley, Ph.D. – Postsecondary Branch Chief and
Acting Associate Commissioner Administrative Data
Division

2:25–2:30   Recap and Adjourn

**DEVELOPMENT OF A PLAN TO PROMOTE DEFENSE
RESEARCH AT HISTORICALLY BLACK COLLEGES AND
UNIVERSITIES, TRIBAL COLLEGES AND UNIVERSITIES,
AND HISPANIC-SERVING INSTITUTIONS—
COMMITTEE MEETING OPEN SESSION—
DOD ASSESSMENT GATHERING SESSION 1**

Virtual

December 1, 2023

1:00–1:05	Welcome
	Committee Members
1:05–1:40	Student support program
	Howard Hughes Medical Institute **Sarah Simmons, Ph.D.** – Director, Grants Management; Program Lead, Driving Change
1:40–1:45	Recap and Adjourn

DEVELOPMENT OF A PLAN TO PROMOTE DEFENSE RESEARCH AT HISTORICALLY BLACK COLLEGES AND UNIVERSITIES, TRIBAL COLLEGES AND UNIVERSITIES, AND HISPANIC-SERVING INSTITUTIONS— COMMITTEE MEETING OPEN SESSION— DOD ASSESSMENT GATHERING SESSION 2

Virtual

December 8, 2023

12:00–12:05   Welcome

Committee Members

12:05–12:40   Federal Research Engagement Programs

National Aeronautics and Space Administration
Patricia Boyd, Ph.D. – NASA's Research Initiation Awards/NASA SMD Bridge Seed Funding Program

12:40–1:20   Federal Development Program

Regional Technology and Innovation Hubs
Eric Smith, Esq – Program Director
Annie Colarusso – Deputy Program Director

1:20–1:25   Recap and Adjourn

**DEVELOPMENT OF A PLAN TO PROMOTE DEFENSE
RESEARCH AT HISTORICALLY BLACK COLLEGES AND
UNIVERSITIES, TRIBAL COLLEGES AND UNIVERSITIES,
AND HISPANIC-SERVING INSTITUTIONS—
SITE VISIT**

California State University, Bakersfield
9001 Stockdale Highway
Bakersfield, CA 93311

January 23-24, 2024

DAY 1 (PST)

9:30–10:00   Welcome and Introductions (Office of the President, Horace Mitchell Conference Room)

Kristen Watson, EdD, Chief of Staff to the President
Andrea Christelle, Ph.D. – Committee Co-Chair
André Porter, MS – Study Director

10:00–11:00 Meeting and Discussion with CSUB Interim President (Office of the President, Horace Mitchell Conference Room)

Vernon Harper, Ph.D., CSUB Interim President
James Rodriguez, Ph.D., CSUB Interim Provost, Committee members

11:00–11:20 Break

11:20–3:45   Tour of Facilities and Departments
- Question themes:
  - o Describe the barriers that your institution encounters as it pursues increased research engagement.
  - o Legislative engagement/strategy
  - o Describe your current infrastructure and the components required to support/grow your institution's research capabilities. (Personnel, facilities, administration, etc.)

  o Of what work are you most proud? How to engage DOD in the strategic advantage of advancing this research?
  o Where would you like to engage but lack resources?

11:20–12:30 Department and Laboratories (RM: various)
- School of Natural Sciences, Mathematics, and Engineering
- Department of Biology
- Department of Chemistry and Biochemistry
- Department of Computer & Electrical Engineering & Computer Science
- Department of Geological Sciences
- Department of Physics and Engineering Nursing Simulation Lab
- Fab Lab

Committee members
Karlo Lopez, Ph.D., Associate Dean, Natural Sciences, Mathematics, and Engineering (NSME)
Kristen Watson, EdD, Chief of Staff to the President

12:30–1:30 WORKING LUNCH - CSUB Department Administrators (Office of the President, Horace Mitchell Conference Room)

Committee members
Jane Dong, Ph.D., Dean, NSME
Karlo Lopez, Ph.D., Associate Dean, NSME
Andrea Medina, NSME Director of Grants & Outreach

1:30–1:45 Break

1:45–3:00 Administrative Offices (Office of the President, Horace Mitchell Conference Room)
- Research enterprise units: Finance
- Sponsored Programs Academic Affairs, etc.

Debra Jackson, Ph.D., AVP for Academic Affairs, Dean of Academic Programs
Isabel Sumaya, Ph.D., Interim AVP, Grants Research and Sponsored Programs
Jane Dong, Ph.D., Dean, NSME

3:00–3:45   Technology Transfer Capacity/Resources (Office of the President, Horace Mitchell Conference Room)

CSUB Department Administrators
Committee members

DAY 1 ADJOURNS

DAY 2

9:00–10:30   Welcome and Student/Faculty Research Presentations/ Posters (RM: Student Union - MPR)

Kristen Watson, EdD, Chief of Staff to the President
CSUB Faculty/students
Committee members

10:30–12:00 Faculty/Student/Administrator Panel (RM: Student Union – MPR)

CSUB Faculty/students
Committee members

12:00–12:30 Committee Debrief

DAY 2 ADJOURNS

Appendix B

Committee Biographical Sketches

Andrea Christelle, Ph.D., (*Co-chair*) is the vice provost for research at Diné College, where she fosters innovation and knowledge generation rooted in Diné values. She previously served as the acting director of Good Systems, an AI Grand Challenge at the University of Texas at Austin, and as the founding director of Philosophy in the Public Interest at Northern Arizona University.

Dr. Christelle's expertise lies in promoting and encouraging new knowledge frameworks in research and beyond. She is a diversity, equity, and inclusion committee member for the National Council of University Research Administrators, Region VII, and serves on the editorial advisory board of the *Public Philosophy Journal*. Dr. Christelle is the recipient of the civic leadership award for the League of Women Voters, Greater Verde Valley, and the American Philosophical Association/Philosophy Documentation Center's Award for Excellence and Innovation in Philosophy Programs. She is a founder of Sedona Philosophy, a unique tour company that combines immersion in the natural world with philosophical reflection to advance discovery through experience and observation.

Dr. Christelle has a Ph.D. in philosophy from Tulane University and a diverse background in higher education administration, economic development, AI ethics, and public philosophy.

Erin Lynch, Ph.D., C.R.A., (*Co-chair*) is the president of Quality Education for Minorities Network. Dr. Lynch's research area is strategic planning and program development. Her work focuses on Historically Black Colleges and Universities (HBCUs), research cultivation, educational assessment, program evaluation, and campus climate assessments. She is formerly associate provost of scholarship, research, and innovation and dean of Graduate School and endowed professor of education at Winston-Salem State University, a North Carolina HBCU; research director of the Center of Excellence of Learning Sciences at Tennessee State University; and faculty member in the College of Education and director of Office of Undergraduate Research at Austin Peay State University.

She was a 2020 Woodson Fund HBCU Change Makers Award recipient and a 2016 Excellence in Presentation Awardee at the Academic Business World and International Conference on Learning and Administration in Higher Education conferences for her work entitled "Black Minds Matter: The Call to Retention of Young Black Academics (YBAs) in Higher Education." She has a B.A. in English/secondary education from James Madison University, an Ma.ED. in special education from Vanderbilt University, an Ed.D. in curriculum and instruction from Tennessee State University, and a Ph.D. in industrial organizational psychology from Northcentral University.

Nadya T. Bliss, Ph.D., is the executive director of the Global Security Initiative at Arizona State University (ASU). In this capacity, she leads a pan-university organization advancing research, education, and other programming in support of national and global security. Before joining ASU, Bliss spent 10 years at the Massachusetts Institute of Technology (MIT) Lincoln Laboratory, most recently as the founding group leader of the Computing and Analytics Group.

Actively involved in national service, she is the chair of the Defense Advanced Research Projects Agency Information Science and Technology Study Group, and the vice-chair of the Computing Community Consortium. She also serves on the National Academies of Sciences, Engineering, and Medicine's Cyber Resilience Forum and the National Academies' Climate Security Roundtable.

Dr. Bliss is the recipient of the inaugural (2011) MIT Lincoln Laboratory Early Career Technical Achievement award and the R&D100 award for her work on PVTOL: Parallel Vector Tile Optimizing Library. She received bachelor's and master's degrees in computer science from Cornell University and earned her doctorate in applied mathematics for the life and social sciences (complex adaptive systems science) from ASU.

Robert D. Braun, Ph.D., (NAE) is head of the Space Exploration Sector at the Johns Hopkins Applied Physics Laboratory, with responsibilities that span all civil and national security space activities at the lab. He has contributed to the formulation, development, and operation of multiple spaceflight missions and is a recognized authority in hypersonics technology and the development of entry, descent, and landing systems. Dr. Braun previously served in executive positions at the Jet Propulsion Laboratory, the University of Colorado Boulder (CU Boulder), and National Aeronautics and Space Administration, and has served as a tenured professor at Georgia Tech, CU Boulder, and Caltech.

He earned a B.S. in aerospace engineering from Pennsylvania State University, an M.S. in astronautics from George Washington University, and a Ph.D. in aeronautics and astronautics from Stanford University. He is a member of the National Academy of Engineering, a fellow of the American Institute of Aeronautics and Astronautics and the American Astronomical Society, and the author or coauthor of over 300 technical publications.

Brian K. Chappell, Ph.D., is a research staff member on the Nuclear Weapons Strategy and Policy Team and serves as vice chair of the Black Professionals Employee Resource Group at the Institute for Defense Analyses. Dr. Chappell retired from the U.S. Air Force (USAF) as a Lieutenant Colonel in 2021, after serving 28 years on active duty. He is a veteran of the Afghanistan War and a career Minuteman III Intercontinental Ballistic Missile nuclear weapons launch officer. While assigned to the Pentagon, Dr. Chappell served as a Middle East Policy Senior Advisor to the Under Secretary of the Air Force for International Affairs, South Asia Policy Advisor to the Chairman of the Joint Chiefs of Staff, and a Senior Advisor for Defense Governance to the Under Secretary of Defense for Policy.

While on active duty, Dr. Chappell led the Office of the Under Secretary of Defense for Policy's oversight of five academic Regional Centers and their $58 million budget and managed the Air Force Culture and Language Center's $7 million culture training contracts. Dr. Chappell led two Air Advisor Review Teams to Iraq and one to Afghanistan to interview USAF personnel and identify future Security Cooperation training requirements. He also worked with the defense industry business development teams and as the country director for the $2 billion United Arab Emirates foreign military sales portfolio, and led oversight of USAF fiscal year programming for out-year international education and training allocations.

Dr. Chappell is the author of *State Responses to Nuclear Proliferation: The Differential Effects of Threat Perception.* He is a member of Phi Beta Delta Honor Society for International Scholars, Pi Lambda Theta National Honor Society in Education, The National Honor Society of Phi Kappa Phi, and Pi Sigma Alpha National Political Science Honor Society. He is also the inaugural recipient of the Monroe High School (MI) Distinguished Alumni Award. Dr. Chappell is a life member of the Veterans of Foreign Wars and Kappa Alpha Psi Fraternity, and is a graduate of the Air War College, Air Command and Staff College, National Intelligence University's Post-Graduate Intelligence Program, and Harvard Kennedy School Executive Education Course on Leadership in Crises. Dr. Chappell earned a B.A. in political science from the University of Michigan, Ann Arbor; an M.S. in administration from Central Michigan University; an M.A. in international affairs from Catholic University; an M.S. in strategic intelligence from the National Intelligence University; and a Ph.D. in world politics from Catholic University.

Paul T. Deaderick is a senior project leader for the Aerospace Corporation and leads Satellite Systems and Ground Systems Integration and Test, and Transition to Operations. As a Federally Funded Research and Development Center professional, Mr. Deaderick is a seasoned satellite operator and engineering expert with over 30 years of diverse expertise across government, military and commercial aerospace, IT, and communications infrastructure construction management. Mr. Deaderick actively works with Next Generation Geostationary and Polar Overhead Persistent Infrared, Medium Earth Orbit, and Low Earth Orbit Overhead Persistent Infrared programs.

During his prior assignment, Mr. Deaderick served at the National Reconnaissance Office and led Continuity of Operations, the Crisis Response Cell, and Intelligence Oversight programs. To fill a critical gap, Mr. Deaderick served as the interim chief of staff to the Aerospace Data Facility-Colorado Commander and deputy in the daily operations of the largest multi-mission ground station responsible for supporting worldwide defense operations and multi-agency collection, analysis, reporting, and dissemination of intelligence information. In a prior assignment as a senior intelligence officer, he developed and delivered critical intelligence to customers ranging from deployed personnel to national level policymakers. Mr. Deaderick has been a systems engineering branch chief, a command briefer, and the author of several intelligence community white papers on coalition leadership in a multi-agency multi-intelligence environment.

Mr. Deaderick is a retired Lieutenant Colonel who served over 30 years on active duty and in the Reserves in the Colorado and Ohio Air National Guard. He earned his B.S. in electronic engineering technology from Metropolitan State University of Denver and his M.S. in space systems operations management from Webster University.

Mr. Deaderick served on the Metropolitan State University Applied Engineering Sciences Advisory Council and has been an industry speaker for the University of Colorado, Colorado Springs, and Colorado State University Global. He is a member of the National Society of Black Engineers, American Institute of Aerospace and Astronautics (Diversity Chair), the Colorado Space Coalition, the Society of Physician Entrepreneurs, and Colorado Space Business Round Table (Advisory Board).

Bruce H. Dunson, Ph.D., is the president of Metrica, Inc. He oversees the operational, financial, and contracting units of Metrica and its subsidiaries and affiliates: Metrica Relocations+ Inc., Traclabs, Inc., and Pride Automation, Inc. Traclabs conducts Small Business Innovation Research-award-winning research on robotics, automation, and artificial intelligence. In past decades, Dr. Dunson served as associate professor and chairman of the Department of Economics and Finance at Prairie View A&M University, assistant professor and adjunct associate professor at Texas A&M University, and assistant professor at the University of Maryland.

He has over 35 years' experience in managing and conducting research in the area of applied microeconomics and in the analysis of data using statistical methods. Dr. Dunson spent the early part of his career working simultaneously in academia and the government sector, conducting economic research for the Department of Defense, the National Science Foundation, and other federal government agencies. His relevant technical expertise includes econometric analysis, survey design, cost benefit analysis, program evaluation, and economic analysis. Previously, he earned his bachelor's degree (political science, University of California, Irvine, 1969), master's degrees (city and regional planning, University of California, Berkeley, 1971; economics, Harvard, 1976), and Ph.D. (economics, Harvard, 1979).

Erick C. Jones, Ph.D., former dean, College of Engineering, at University of Nevada, Reno. He is a former senior science advisor in the Office of the Chief Economist at the U.S. State Department. He is a former professor and associate dean for graduate studies at the College of Engineering at the

University of Texas at Arlington. Dr. Jones is an internationally recognized researcher in industrial manufacturing and systems engineering.

His career over the past 25 years has spanned industry, government, and academia. His current research on pandemic supply chains was a main consideration for working at the State Department, in the Office of the Chief Economist. Dr. Jones studies how the United States can better understand the economics of supply chains and how their disruptions impact global commerce, operations, and quality of life.

Keith A. McGee, Ph.D., is professor of biology at Alcorn State University. A native of Quitman, located in Clarke County, MS, he began his postsecondary education at Mississippi Valley State University, majoring in biology. He received a Ph.D. from the University of Southern Mississippi in molecular biology. Dr. McGee's research focused on a family of ATP transport proteins, specifically those involved in phenotypic multi-drug resistance. As a faculty member, he sustained a productive graduate student training program, advising many master's-degree seeking students, along with many undergraduates and summer research students.

Dr. McGee has served in multiple administrative capacities at Alcorn State University; most recently he was appointed to serve as the inaugural associate provost for research, innovation, and graduate education. In this role, Dr. McGee is responsible for providing leadership in developing a clear research vision for the university, while growing its research footprint, and elevating interdisciplinary research activities. He is charged with promoting an understanding and drive for new research opportunities, working with the university deans on all aspects of research and graduate education to ensure alignment with their specific disciplines, while supporting and expanding innovative graduate programs and scholarly activity.

Eric R. Muth, Ph.D., is vice chancellor for research and economic development at North Carolina Agricultural and Technical State University, with the goal of helping others grow their research acumen and programs. He is trained as an experimental psychologist and has over 25 years' experience post-degree leading a wide variety of research and development projects in both the laboratory and the field. Dr. Muth spent 3 years as a uniformed researcher in the U.S. Navy and performed data collection aboard ship, in aircraft, and in virtual environments. Dr. Muth spent 19 years of his career at Clemson University and has been associated with over $7 million of funded research and 100 publications, with the last portion of his career working on translational research in the area of mobile health technologies.

Dr. Muth's graduate training was in gastrointestinal psychophysiology. He completed his dissertation at the Pennsylvania State University Hershey Medical Center. His dissertation and early publications were related to functional gastrointestinal disorders. From August 2008 to 2009, Dr. Muth spent the year on sabbatical in Germany, funded on a Humboldt Research Fellowship working at the Universität Tübingen in the Psychosomatic Medicine Department. There he continued working on projects associated with functional gastrointestinal disorders and obesity. In 2019, he was accepted as a member of the Academy of Behavioral Medicine Research. In addition to his behavioral medicine work, Dr. Muth is an internationally known expert in the area of motion sickness. His work over the years in this area focused on understanding the causes, symptoms, physiology, and prevention of motion sickness, with specific attention on user experience and performance while wearing head-mounted displays.

Anna Quider, Ph.D., is founder and principal of the Quider Group and an affiliated senior research fellow at Northern Illinois University (NIU). As assistant vice president for federal relations at NIU, she developed and championed policies to increase equity in the federal science and technology (S&T) research enterprise for historically underrepresented groups and emerging research institutions. She was president of the Science Coalition, a national coalition of research universities supporting federal S&T research, and held research and policy leadership positions within the Association of Public and Land-grant Universities.

Prior to NIU, Dr. Quider developed S&T policies and programs at the U.S. Department of State and the U.S. House of Representatives. Dr. Quider is a fellow of the American Physical Society (APS) and chair-elect of the APS Forum on Physics and Society. Appointed by the UK Ambassador to the United States, she is the lead science, technology, engineering, and mathematics evaluator for the Marshall Scholarship at the British Embassy. Dr. Quider holds a Ph.D. in astronomy from the University of Cambridge, where she was a Marshall Scholar. She holds a B.S. with Honors in physics in astronomy and a B.A. with dual majors in religious studies and the history and philosophy of science from the University of Pittsburgh.

Aaron M. Schutt is president and CEO of Doyon, Limited. He is responsible for working with the board of directors to set the overall direction of the Doyon Family of Companies and provide leadership to its senior management team. Mr. Schutt has worked at Doyon since 2006. Prior to being named president and CEO, Schutt served as senior vice president and chief operating officer from 2008 to 2011.

Mr. Schutt clerked for Alaska Supreme Court Justice Alexander Bryner after receiving his juris doctorate from Stanford Law School. He holds a Master of Science in civil engineering from Stanford University and graduated with honors and as an S. Town Stephenson scholar from Washington State University with a Bachelor of Science in civil engineering. Before joining Doyon in 2006, he was an attorney at the Anchorage offices of national law firms Sonosky, Chambers, Sachse, Miller & Munson, LLP, and Heller Ehrman, LLP, where he represented tribal and Alaska Native Claims Settlement Act corporation clients in transactional and business matters.

He serves on the board of directors for Northrim BanCorp, Inc., and Akeela, Inc., and on the University of Alaska Fairbanks Board of Advisors. In 2004, Mr. Schutt was named as a recipient of the *Alaska Journal of Commerce*'s "Top 40 Under 40" award.

Mr. Schutt is Koyukon Athabascan and is an enrolled member of the Native Village of Tanana.

Sharon Tettegah, Ph.D., is professor and director of the Center for Black Studies Research at the University of California, Santa Barbara. Her research framework is at the intersection of science, technology, engineering, and mathematics (STEM); psychology; and education with an emphasis on Black and ethnic studies. Her current research focuses on the use of high-performance computing to examine broadening participation in STEM and beyond.

The focus of Dr. Tettegah's most recent past research examines affective, behavioral, and cognitive facets of empathy and empathic dispositions using multiple technologies (e.g., functional magnetic resonance imaging, simulations, games). Her interest and research in empathy, emotions, and technology is the result of passion and commitment to the improvement of equity in leadership, teaching, and learning.

In addition to her research on empathy, Dr. Tettegah is also involved in the examination of innovation and creativity in STEM fields. Her goals as a researcher and practitioner are to broaden participation for students of color in STEM disciplines.

Dr. Tettegah's portfolio includes leadership roles as associate dean for research and sponsored programs in the College of Education at the

University of Nevada, Las Vegas; former National Science Foundation Program Officer, where she managed programs in the Division of Research on Learning and Computer and Information Science and Engineering; and chair of the American Psychological Association's Continuing Education Committee. She also had a Gubernatorial Appointment as a member of California's Interagency Council on Early Intervention, served as chair of the Committee for Early Career Psychologists, and served as treasurer elect at the American Psychological Association's Division 15. Dr. Tettegah is also a faculty affiliate with the Center for Responsible Machine Learning and Center for Information Technology and Society.

C. Reynold Verret, Ph.D., is the sixth president of Xavier University of Louisiana. Prior to his 2015 investiture as president, Dr. Verret served as provost and chief academic officer for Savannah State University. Previously, he served as provost at Wilkes University in Pennsylvania and as dean and professor of chemistry and biochemistry at University of the Sciences in Philadelphia. Dr. Verret also served on faculty at Tulane University and Clark Atlanta University. Dr. Verret's research interests have included the cytotoxicity of immune cells, biosensors, and biomarkers. He has published in the fields of biochemistry and immunology, and also collaborated on matters of social exclusion and health. Throughout, Dr. Verret has worked to increase the number of U.S. students pursuing degrees in science, technology, engineering, and mathematics disciplines and continuing to advanced study. This includes the development of qualified science and math teachers in K-12. Dr. Verret received his undergraduate degree cum laude in biochemistry from Columbia University and a Ph.D. in bio-chemistry from the Massachusetts Institute of Technology. To these, he added postdoctoral experiences as fellow at the Howard Hughes Institute for Immunology at Yale University and the Center for Cancer Research at Massachusetts Institute of Technology.

Appendix C

Section 233 of Relevant NDAA Legislation

SEC. 233. REPORT ON EFFORTS TO INCREASE THE
PARTICIPATION OF HISTORICALLY BLACK COLLEGES
AND UNIVERSITIES AND OTHER MINORITY-
SERVING INSTITUTIONS IN THE RESEARCH AND
DEVELOPMENT ACTIVITIES OF THE DEPARTMENT
OF DEFENSE.

(a) Report Required.--Not later than 180 days after the date of the enactment of this Act, the Under Secretary of Defense for Research and Engineering shall submit to the congressional defense committees a report on measures that may be implemented to increase the participation of historically Black colleges and universities and other minority-serving institutions in the research, development, test, and evaluation activities of the Department of Defense.

(b) Elements.--The report under subsection (a) shall include the following:

(1) A strategy for the provision of long-term institutional support to historically Black colleges and universities and other minority-serving institutions, including support for--

(A) the development and enhancement of the physical research infrastructure of such institutions; and

(B) the research activities of such institutions.

(2) An evaluation of the feasibility of expanding the support provided by the Department of Defense to historically Black colleges and universities and other minority-serving institutions to include support for the development or enhancement of grant and contract administration capabilities at such institutions.

(3) An evaluation of options to strengthen support for historically Black colleges and universities and other minority-serving institutions within the military departments and other organizations and elements of the Department, including an evaluation of the need for and feasibility of establishing dedicated organizations within the Army, Navy, Marine Corps, Air Force, and Space Force to increase engagement with such institutions.

(4) A review of the adequacy of the level of staffing within the Department that is dedicated to engagement with historically Black colleges and universities and other minority-serving institutions.

(5) A plan to improve data collection and evaluation with respect to historically Black colleges and universities and other minority-serving institutions, including--

(A) harmonization of standards with respect to the type, detail, and organization of data on such institutions;

(B) improving the completeness of data submissions regarding such institutions;

(C) improving the retention of data on such institutions across the Department;

(D) additional data collection specific to such institutions, including data on--

(i) the rates at which such institutions submit proposals for grants and contracts from the Department, the success rates of such proposals, and feedback regarding such proposals;

(ii) the total number of grants and contracts for which such institutions are eligible to apply and the number of applications received from such institutions for such grants and contracts; and

(iii) formal feedback mechanisms for rejected proposals from first-time applicants from such institutions; and

(E) as necessary, promulgation of additional or modified regulations, instructions, or guidance regarding the collection, evaluation, and retention of data on such institutions.

(6) Identification of the types of research facilities, personnel, capabilities, and subject areas that are in-demand within the Department so that historically Black colleges and universities and other minority-serving institutions may prioritize investment in those types of facilities, personnel, capabilities, and subject areas as appropriate.

(7) Identification of metrics that may be used to evaluate, track, and improve the competitiveness of historically Black colleges and universities and other minority-serving institutions for grants and contracts with the Department.

(8) An evaluation of options to implement criteria for the award of grants and contracts that assign value to the inclusion of historically Black colleges and universities and other minority-serving institutions as research partners, including such mechanisms as weighted grant solicitation evaluation criteria and longer periods of performance to allow for capacity-building within such institutions.

(9) An evaluation of options to incentivize the defense industry to support capacity building within historically Black colleges and universities and other minority-serving institutions, including through the incentivization of independent research and development or other activities.

(10) A plan to compile and maintain data regarding institutions of higher education, including historically Black colleges and universities and other minority-serving institutions, that receive funding from departments and agencies of the Federal Government outside the Department of Defense.

(11) A review of the programs and practices of departments and agencies of the Federal Government outside the Department of Defense relevant to increasing research capacity at historically Black colleges and universities and other minority-serving institutions for purposes of--

(A) the potential adoption of best practices within the Department;

(B) the identification of opportunities to leverage the research capacity of such institutions; and

(C) increasing the level of collaboration between the Department and such institutions.

(12) Recommendations for the modification or expansion of the workforce development programs of the Department, including

fellowships and internships, to increase the proportion of the workforce hired from historically Black colleges and universities and other minority-serving institutions.

(13) Such other recommendations as the Under Secretary of Defense for Research and Engineering determines appropriate.

(14) A plan for the implementation of the recommendations included in the report, as appropriate, including an explanation of any additional funding, authorities, or organizational changes needed for the implementation of such recommendations.

(c) Definitions.--In this section:

(1) The term "historically Black college or university" means a part B institution (as defined in section 322 of the Higher Education Act of 1965 (20 U.S.C. 1061)).

(2) The term "institution of higher education" has the meaning given that term in section 101 of the Higher Education Act of 1932 (20 U.S.C. 1001).

(3) The term "other minority-serving institution" means an institution of higher education specified in paragraphs (2) through (7) of section 371(a) of the Higher Education Act of 1965 (20 U.S.C. 1067q(a)).

(d) Report on Implementation.--Not later than 180 days after the date of the submission of the report under subsection (a), the Under Secretary of Defense for Research and Engineering shall submit to the congressional defense committees a report on the progress of the Under Secretary in implementing measures to increase the participation of historically Black colleges and universities and other minority-serving institutions in the research, development, test, and evaluation activities of the Department of Defense, as identified in the report under subsection (a).